T0328003

ENLIVENMENT

UNTIMELY MEDITATIONS

ENLIVENMENT

TOWARD A POETICS FOR THE ANTHROPOCENE

ANDREAS WEBER

THE MIT PRESS
CAMBRIDGE, MASSACHUSETTS
LONDON, ENGLAND

Originally published as *Enlivenment: Eine Kultur des Lebens: Versuch einer Poetik für das Anthropozän* in the series *Fröhliche Wissenschaft* by Matthes & Seitz Berlin: © Matthes & Seitz Berlin Verlagsgesellschaft mbH, Berlin 2016.

This book was set in PF DinText Pro by Toppan Best-set Premedia Limited. Printed and bound in the United States of America.

Library of Congress Cataloging-in-Publication Data

Names: Weber, Andreas, 1967– author.
Title: Enlivenment : toward a poetics for the anthropocene / Andreas Weber.
Description: Cambridge, MA : MIT Press, 2019. | Series: Untimely meditations; 16 | Includes bibliographical references.
Identifiers: LCCN 2018030684 | ISBN 9780262536660 (pbk. : alk. paper)
Subjects: LCSH: Philosophy of nature. | Human ecology.
Classification: LCC BD581 .W3585 2019 | DDC 113—dc23 LC record available at https://lccn.loc.gov/2018030684

10 9 8 7 6 5 4 3

Love is everywhere distinguished from its false semblances by the way in which one respects the independent reality of what one loves.

Raimond Gaita, *The Philosopher's Dog*

Only the mountain has lived long enough to listen objectively to the howl of a wolf.

Aldo Leopold, "Marshland Elegy"

CONTENTS

ACKNOWLEDGMENTS

Many ideas in this book have their origin in fruitful meetings of my own research into biology as a story of unfolding relations and existential issues with a group of highly innovative commons activists and philosophers, at a time that in the future might be recalled as the heyday of Berlin commons thinking between 2010 and 2018. I am particularly grateful to Heike Löschmann (who coined the term *enlivenment*) and to David Bollier, who encouraged me to pursue my thoughts in English and opened some vital doors allowing me to do so, and hence, makes me experience commoning in a real sense. I am happy that Hildegard Kurt has been a companion on that track ever since, in various settings and projects—in a common search for new cultures of aliveness and for an ontology where self comes about through the blossoming of the other, and the other through the full realization of self. This is the ontology we already know through our bodies, and as commoners in a vast circle of giving, that of the ecosystem. It is with Alessandra Weber that I explore how it feels "being" the ecology. I am grateful for sharing on a daily basis how the leaves unfold and the opening buds crackle, and that commoning ultimately is a process of love.

INTRODUCTION: A POETICS OF THE REAL

This essay proposes a new perspective on humans' relation with the sphere we commonly call nature. Throughout this book, I will approach both humans and nature in a way that dissolves the separation between the two categories. I will explore how we can begin to view all beings as participants in a common household of matter, desire, and imagination—an economy of metabolic and poetic transformations. I call this perspective *enlivenment*.

Every living being's identity unfolds as a transformation of the other through one's own self. This self emerges through perceptions and through being touched, through sensual exchanges, through symbols and metaphors, and through the impact of molecules and light, all of which somehow transfer their relevance to the ongoing self-creation of the body. All life, from its very beginning, is made up of such mutual transformations. Our existence in an ecosphere pervaded with life takes part in a vast commons even before we perceive our individuality. All subjectivity is already intersubjectivity. Self is self-through-other.

Each individual belongs to the world and is at the same time an owner of this world—an owner of this rough stone flecked by the waves, ruffled by the wind, caressed by gleams of light. All perception is a commons: a dance of interdependency with the world. The world belongs to us entirely, and at the same time, we are fully entrusted to it. It is only through this give-and-take that we become conscious of it and of ourselves. It is only through honoring this give-and-take in a manner that provides life that we can build our place in the world. This is the principle of embodied identity and of householding.

In what follows, I will develop a set of alternatives to some of the basic assumptions underlying our current worldview. In doing so, I will engage with the Anthropocene debate, and try to recalibrate its basic tendency to view our epoch as the beginning of a human-dominated Earth, in which our species de facto controls everything and humankind and nature are separated in principle but stand on the same level.

The idea of the Anthropocene is that we are living in a new geological era in which human culture has largely overtaken the biogeochemical realities of the earthly household; humans now dominate and control matter, energy streams, and the distribution and existence of biological species. The difference between humans and nature has been claimed to be resolved—not by recognizing that all living beings and living systems are subject to the same natural dynamics and creative principles, but by declaring that humans can assert mastery over all inanimate and animate nature on earth. In this way, the idea of the Anthropocene has overcome the dualism that has defined our culture at least for five hundred if not two thousand years. This is an epochal move, but it is one that could very well go in the wrong direction.

This essay is an attempt to imagine the end of dualism in a different way. It tries to dissolve the opposition between humankind and nature not by understanding all nature as something to be controlled, as something that lends itself to cultural practices because it has the same deep setup as human technology: a purpose-free process of emerging efficiency and optimization. Rather, I propose we understand the identity of humans and nature through a commons of creative transformation that underlies all reality and finds a particularly forceful expression in life. I argue that there can be no dualism, because the fundamental dimension of existence is already shared: it is *aliveness*, the desire to connect through touch and body in order to create fertile communities of mutual flourishing, the members of which experience their identities as selves.

Concerning the Anthropocene, I agree with the poet and ecophilosopher Gary Snyder that the "'wild' is process, as it happens outside human agency, although it might happen inside ourselves. As far as science can reach, it will never get to the bottom of it, because mind, imagination, digestion, breathing, dreaming, loving, and both birth and death are all part of the wild. There will never be an Anthropocene."[1] In addition to realizing how far human influences have pervaded nature, we also need to imagine the wild in ourselves.

All human transactions and our imagination as a whole are fundamentally entangled with nature. They are manifestations of an uncontainable wildness, of a poetic and productive self-organization that simply cannot submit to control or stewardship. Control is a fiction. It is impossible because the uncontainable wild of which Snyder speaks—the associations of fantasy, digestion, the complexity of language, the absoluteness of emotions and instincts—provides the very instruments with which we strive to achieve control.

The commons of reality is a meshwork of affiliations through which aliveness unfolds in ecosystems and history. The commons of reality bears the aliveness of biological and human communities from a perspective of metabolic dependency, the exchange of gifts, and the entanglement of actors through their desire to connect with each other and their need to survive. Living agents bring each other into being by establishing relationships (be they metabolic, predator/prey, or social) and by doing so produce not only their environments but their very identities.[2]

The commons describes an ontology of relations that is at once existential, economic, and ecological. It emphasizes a process of transformation and identity formation that arises out of a mutual relationship that is not only material but experiential. For humans, this ontology produces meaning and emotional reality. For the biosphere, humans included, it produces the energy necessary for life.

I am using the term *commons* to stand for relationships of reciprocity and mutual co-creation.[3] *Commons* is an economics term that relates to a particular organization of livelihood in which there are no users and resources but only diverse participants in a fertile system, which they treat in accordance with a higher goal: that it continue to give life.

The term *commons* characterizes a form of socioeconomy that integrates material and emotional relationships. It is based on the exchange of goods, but also on transformations of meaning. Historically, the commons are a stretch of nature that is used and protected by a certain group of humans, like the rural commons of medieval Britain, where peasants had their cattle graze according to a complex set of rules that granted access to all and prohibited overuse by some.

Today, we see remnants throughout the world of this way of relating to the biosphere and to one another, be it in the commons of the Alpine meadows, the irrigation systems of South America, or the way the San of Southern Africa distribute their hunted-down prey. Commons economies dominate the subsistence economies of rural people in many places throughout the world. It has been the predominant form of livelihood since the dawn of premodern humans at least a million years ago. Its primal characteristic is that it does not distinguish between users and objects, but binds all agents together in a vast interconnected network of giving and receiving, which is meant to create the greatest possible fertility for all. Commons are creating a world of togetherness through mutual transformation.

This fertility is not merely exterior, but also an emotional experience. In traditional commons settings, this emotional dimension is revered explicitly through celebrations and rituals. Commons are about protecting aliveness through participation and reciprocity. They are a way of imagining our ecological role by giving the ecosystem more life. Reality as a whole can be seen as a vast commons, which comes about through the participation of all beings, including human beings. Experiencing membership in this commons from the inside, feeling a relationship with other members and sharing the profound identity of this world, is the unique feeling of being alive. Commons economy therefore establishes the human ecological niche through cultural means.

In this essay, I will paint a picture in which reality thrives through the entanglement of *all* humans, *all* creatures, and the physical, material agents involved in the exchange processes of reality, such as water, rocks, and air. To do this, it will be necessary to do away with the customary notions of "culture" and "nature," which modernity has invariably regarded as detached and divergent. But these two dimensions involve de facto the same entanglement of matter with symbolic meaning. To see this, we need to understand that aliveness is the unfolding, critical connecting element of reality. Aliveness is intrinsic to all social and biological processes and to the cosmos as a biogeochemical whole.[4] They are all driven by an inherent desire for connection, self-realization, and transformation. Aliveness has an objective, empirical substance (in the bodies of the world's beings) and a subjective, tangible dimension (in our own bodies). Aliveness is always interweaving dimensions of matter with perception and experience; it is from the very first cell rife with those dimensions we normally reserve for culture: meaning and expression.

It is essential that we supplement the current mainstream understanding of the Anthropocene from the standpoint of an ontology of the commons. Without this perspective to complete the picture, the Anthropocene—the novel epoch characterized by the supremacy of human beings—would neglect a fundamental element of reality. At present, I am concerned that the idea so predominant in the Anthropocene approach—that we can reconcile humankind with the unconscious, organic in itself and in others (human and not human) by subverting all of this under the power of culture—is just another attempt at domestication. We can see in it one more claim for controlling the world.

CULTURE AS CONTROL

Today, this control is predominantly exerted through the economy. The neoliberal market system and its prerequisite, the separation of resources (which are traded) and subjects (who trade these resources in order to allocate them), are products of the historical Enlightenment. They follow its method of exerting control by dividing the world into two halves: one nonliving sphere that needs to be colonized, and one that oversees and manages this control. The world, however, becomes better not through control, but through participation.

We will only be able to survive the Anthropocene and change it into a more productive way of dealing with our own humanity and the biosphere if we understand that humans do not pervade and influence nature alone. Instead, the human sphere is constituted and filled by something that cannot be submitted to cultural control and management, because it nourishes our identity on a deep level: our self-organizing, irreducible aliveness, which flows into the reality of ecosystems, emotional impulses, and poetic imagination.

The Anthropocene approach lacks the awareness that it is *mutuality* that ignites our aliveness, even though we do not understand it. It does not grasp that there are always two sides to any exchange, be it of things (in the economy), of meanings (in biological communication or human expressivity), or of identities (in the bonding between two subjects). It has an exterior, material dimension, but also an inner, existential aspect in which inwardness comes to the surface. What is missing is the deeply poetic aspect of reality, of any existence in it.

Every process that exists is a way in which a relationship unfolds and conveys meaning: meaning that we—human, animal, plant, and other subjects—experience through our emotions. For this reason we must develop our understanding of a living cosmos, of its natural becoming, its social transformations, and the way in which it provides us our material needs. We can do this in a way that is not automatically reductionist only by means of a poetics. The world is weight and volume, and it is inwardness (or "gravity and grace" as Simone Weil put it),[5] and the latter is only possible through the former. The world is matter desiring to come into contact with other matter, and it creates meaning to the degree to which this desire is realized or not.[6]

This constant drive of things to connect with one another, to become more individual through connections and to be transformed by these connections, and to thereby become more other, more of a "con-division," to take part in a mutual sharing—grants the presence of feeling in the world. If there is a desire to connect, this desire can fail. If there is a possibility of failure, there is meaning: the yearning for blossoming. If there is yearning, this world has an inward side, and as all processes in the world are material, this inward side becomes graspable through matter.

It is the breathing presence of bodies—bodies of rock, water, flesh, and air—that conveys the inwardness of matter to our senses: bodies that are as much "mere matter" as they are a presence of meaning and selfhood. Matter that experiences itself as inwardness through *being* matter: this is a definition of life. Reality is productive and expressive because it is alive. For the most part, current Anthropocene thinking does not grasp this perspective. It tends to overlook what stands in the center of reality as we experience it, and what builds the core of reality: the world's deep aliveness.

The Anthropocene proposes a reconciliation of man and nature. But it will only favor life and lead humankind into a more peaceful way of treating the other if we stop regarding nature as being hopelessly under human control. Instead, we need to grasp that we are ourselves nature, which is to say, we are aliveness—transient transformations in ongoing material and meaningful relationships. This process experiences itself emotionally and unfolds in a fertile way, producing ever more complex degrees of freedom, as well as dependency. This existential process of self-realization is *imagination*, which materially expresses itself.

TECHNÉ OR POIESIS?

After more than three hundred years of Enlightenment-style thinking, the Anthropocene offers us the possibility of moving beyond its fundamental trait of draining material reality of any subjectivity. We now can develop an idea of the intrinsic desire to unfold through touch and transformation within reality. Enlightenment-style thinking can be defined by its omission of what marks life at its very core: the intertwining of matter and desire. For Enlightenment thinking, there is either matter—accounted for in terms of science and technology—or desire—reserved for humans and their endeavors, language, and culture.

Several authors have begun to overcome this dualistic split by imbuing nonhuman beings and even things with agency. This is the task that some proponents of the so-called *new materialism* have embarked on in order to avoid the impasse of a world that lacks life.[7] But the idea of agency is still too shortsighted if we don't explain how agency comes into the world and how the desire for certain aims arises, without which agency makes no sense. Agents have interests, and we need to understand how these interests come about in a cosmos made of matter that does not object to change.

The crucial point to be stressed in this essay, and which is still largely overlooked, is that agency comes with inwardness. Inwardness sets its own values of unfolding, and strives for these values to be met. Life has needs, because it is matter that desires to conserve a specific sense of inwardness. The world is matter, and this matter is always working toward a sentient body that is trying to blossom. Our sense of desire and flourishing is bound into that larger vector, and makes ourselves responsible for the degree to which it unfolds.

We therefore need to supplant the concept of *techné*, which deeply marks the Anthropocene with its optimism toward human stewardship of the Earth, with the concept of *poiesis*. This poiesis is not about a language game. It is rather the element that brings forth reality. Poiesis cannot be shut down. It can only be overlooked or misunderstood in an always painful, and often potentially lethal, way.

We need to comprehend that we live in a world that is not divided into things and ideas, or into resources and consumers, or into culture and nature. Reality arises from the creation of relationships and from continuous fertile transformations. Any thinking in terms of relationship can only come about as a poetics.[8] Any practice of aliveness can only be a poetic practice. What we miss, and what the proponents of the Anthropocene (and its various synonyms, be it "posthumanism," "eco-pragmatism," or "object-oriented ontology") overlook, is a poetics of aliveness. This essay is meant to be a contribution to defining this.

The position taken here will be called *enlivenment*,[9] because its central thesis is that we have to reconsider "life" and "aliveness" as fundamental categories of thought and of practical actions. Enlivenment tries to supplement—not substitute—rational thinking and empirical observation (the core practices of the Enlightenment position) with the "empirical subjectivity" of living beings, and with the "poetic objectivity" of meaningful experiences.

I argue that the greatest obstacle to the vexing questions of sustainability (itself a very elastic term with multiple and conflicting meanings) is the fact that science, society, and politics have for the last two hundred years lost their interest in understanding actual lived and felt embodied existence—that of humans, but also that of other beings. Scientific progress—and all explanations of biological, mental, and social processes—is based on the smallest possible building blocks of matter and systems, and is gained by analyses that presume that evolution in nature is guided by principles of scarcity, competition, and selection of the fittest. To put it in provocative terms, one could say that rational thinking is an ideology that focuses on dead matter. Its premises have no way of comprehending the reality of lived experience. Should it be so surprising, then, that the survival of life on our planet has become the most urgent problem?

Based on new findings predominantly in biology and economics, I propose here a different view. I argue that lived experience, embodied meaning, material exchange, and subjectivity are key factors that cannot be excluded from a scientific picture of the biosphere and its actors. A worldview that can explain the world only in the "third person," as if everything were ultimately a nonliving thing, denies the existence of the very actors who set forth this view. It is a worldview that deliberately ignores the fact that we are subjective, feeling humans—members of an animal species whose living metabolisms are in constant material exchange.

In the vision of the world that I propose here, we human beings are always part and parcel of nature. But this nature is much more like ourselves than we might imagine: It is creative and pulsing with life in every cell. It is creating individual autonomy and freedom by its very constraints. Reality desires—and expresses this desire through the vulnerable bodies of beings.

Because we are living, vulnerable creatures on this animate Earth, we can understand or "feel" nature's forces if only because we are *made* of them. But these principles—the fact that life inevitably comes about through the tendency of matter to diverge, connect, and mutually transform—by no means guarantee an idyllic picture of a benign "Mother Nature" that needs to be protected. Nature's truth lies in its creative openness, which consistently gives life and trades in death, and not in an ostensible wholeness or healthiness. That there is such a truth is authenticated by our own individual experience throughout our lives.

I propose here a new approach to understanding our "sustainability dilemma" by urging that we embrace a new cultural orientation toward the open-ended, embodied, meaning-generating, paradoxical, and inclusive processes of life. To some this may sound as if I am proposing a new naturalism—the view that everything is composed of material entities. But if so, it is a naturalism of a second order that takes into account that nature is not a meaning-free or neutral realm, but is rather a source of existential meaning that is continuously produced by relations between individuals, an unfolding history of freedom.

The following pages are meant as first steps toward exploring the terrain. I will try to substitute the bioeconomic principles that are guiding so many of our economic, political, educational, and private decisions today with new principles of enlivenment. These are based on the observation that we are living in a shared and cocreated biosphere, that we are parts of an unfolding process of natural freedom, and that as humans we are not only capable of directly experiencing this aliveness, but we also need to experience it. The experience of being alive is a basic human requirement that connects us to all living organisms.

Acknowledging this existential need is not only important for the future progress of the life sciences; it is imperative to our future as a species on an endangered planet. Our inability to honor "being alive" as a rich, robust category of thought in critical thinking, economics, public policy, and law means that we do not really understand how to build and maintain a sustainable, life-fostering, enlivened society. It means that we are stuck in a fundamental error about our own deep character, and about that of the cosmos.

FREEDOM AS COMMUNION

Enlivenment is not an arcane historical or philosophical matter but a set of deep principles ordering how we perceive, think, and act. If we can grasp enlivenment as a vision, we can begin to train ourselves to see differently and to approach political struggles and policy with a new perspective. The political consequences of adopting such an approach, which I call an "enlivened policy," a "culture of life," or even a "policy of life," are far-reaching. Only a non-dualistic viewpoint allows for full inclusion and cooperation because there is no disjuncture between rational theory and social practice; the two are intertwined. Existing in reality does not allow for radical disjunctures. Our own existence, in which metabolism and meaning constantly intermingle, is proof of that. Our own existence, if we want to embrace it fully again without the exclusion of undesirable aspects or features that need control or are earmarked for opti-mization, is dependent on our acceptance that our world is not to be taken apart, that every material impact gener-ates meaning, and that every meaning engenders material consequences.

At the same time, I am not proposing a Utopia. On the contrary: I only intend to call for more tenderness toward what is really there. The perspective I am advocating here allows for a deeper acknowledgement of the unavoidable messiness of life—conflicts, bad timing, shortcomings—for which rules of negotiation and accommodation have to be cultivated. In a reality that is massively cocreated through a constant reweaving of relationships and the associated reciprocal transformation, conflicts are not only unavoid-able, they are part and parcel of the way desire manifests itself. These dilemmas ignite between the self and the other, between the good of the whole and one's own well-being, between courage and ecstasy.

These are the fundamental antinomies of existence whose perception led Gershom Scholem to the bold thought of the necessary incompleteness of any creation.[10] There always needs to be negotiation; rules of engagement must be constantly found and cultivated—without ever reaching a state of stability, without ever achieving an optimum. And precisely this is aliveness. The freedom it yearns for does not want to secure and enclose, but to transform constraints into new imaginations.

Freedom has been the grand project of the Enlightenment. The ethos of advancing the individual's personal autonomy, of being one's own master, of emancipating oneself from limitations, still determines much of our world, from our self-image to which political actions are deemed appropriate. The matter at issue is the personal autonomy of the individual, who needs to be his or her own master in order to fulfill his or her own needs in accordance with human dignity. The freedom that enlivenment seeks to advance does not revoke these aims. It rather substitutes them with our freedom as individuals and groups to be "alive-in-connectedness"—the freedom that comes from aligning individual needs and interests with those of the larger community. The self is always a function of the whole: the whole, however, is equally a function of the individual. Only this integrated freedom can provide the power to reconcile humanity with the natural world.

Enlivenment understands freedom as the fertile forming of necessity, which arises from the fact that we are connected to each other as feeling bodies, as individuals, and as groups, and that we stand in mutual exchange with the biosphere. Freedom becomes manifest only when individual needs and interests are imagined together with those of greater communities in a precarious, tense, even paradoxical balance. Only this integrating freedom can unfold the power necessary to reconcile humankind with the natural world.

1 THE IDEOLOGY OF DEATH

The world does not become more alive. The discovery of the Anthropocene, that humankind now rules all global cycles of matter and energy, is just another way of expressing that forty years of sustainability policy have not brought about a breakthrough. They might not even have changed anything at all. Many crises that sustainability was meant to mitigate with a solution-oriented perspective have worsened, even as new ones have arisen.

Species loss, a topic on which we have grown rather numb, has not slowed down, for example, but has instead accelerated into a full-blown "sixth extinction."[1] Global warming, despite all attempts at curtailing it, is speeding up so quickly that it has become difficult to believe it could ever slow down. The depredation of entire landscapes annihilates the subsistence of humans who react with ecologically and economically motivated mass migrations, the scope of which our planet has not seen since the end of antiquity. All these are aspects of a deep-rooted obstacle. Its dimension becomes visible through the career of the term *sustainability* itself: created by Gro Harlem Brundlandt's report to the UN as an ambitious ecosocial concept,[2] it has degraded into a catchword in glossy corporate brochures.

It is important to see not only the external or material aspects of these challenges, but also their more or less hidden, subjective dimensions, which together show that it is aliveness as such that is at stake. Perhaps we need to talk about a "global crisis in sense-making." Its scope encompasses, among other things, the constant dismissal of social achievements that are important for the societal and mental well-being of humans and the solidarity among them, and whose laborious implementation had been the great success of the civil society and the civil rights movement in the decades after World War II until the early 1980s. All this came to a standstill in the mid-1980s, ostensibly because of the impossibility of funding for a more life-centered policy, as some historians have described it. Some scholars, however, regard this development as the systematic takeover of global capital.[3] Capital transforms what is alive into resources that can be sold, and as a result, profound human needs for connection, for personal involvement in the affairs of one's own community, for a true place of one's own, for the experience of identity-in-connection, grow increasingly difficult to satisfy. This loss of fulfillment, which indeed is a loss of true life, is the flip side of the feigned need for efficiency and, more recently, "austerity," which has begun to dominate global social politics.

Another important part of the current crisis is the strange decline in life satisfaction in many industrial countries that comes about with rising material well-being.[4] Part of this is the fact that mental health problems are continuously growing in the worldwide population. Uneasiness and even continuous suffering are the order of the day. According to the World Health Organization (WHO), unipolar depression was "ranked as the third leading cause of the global burden of disease in 2004 and is predicted to move into the second place by 2020, and into the first place by 2030," surpassing infectious and heart diseases and cancer.[5] Depression, however, is directly related to not feeling alive anymore.

The global crisis in sense-making is a fundamental crisis for life on a global scale. It is a crisis for life insofar as lives—individual plant lives, animal lives, and those of entire species—are vanishing daily from the planet, insofar as the human experience of aliveness is severely limited, and insofar as the space we reserve for a concept of aliveness in our worldview is more or less nonexistent. This crisis results from the decades-long attack on the freedom to exist as an individual connected to others. These factors cannot be viewed in isolation from one another, because they are aspects of one and the same problem.

Nonetheless, the standard approach is to separate dilemmas from one another (the species crisis, the education crisis, the financial crisis, and so on). The mainstream treatment of our manifold dilemmas is to sort out various problems in separate "silos" and then search for single, specific "solutions." This procedure amounts to the only officially acceptable methodology in established institutions, whether they are educational institutions or public health systems, environmental organizations or international policy groups. But an analytical approach that separates and externalizes problems to make them technically manageable is precisely why these troubles have arisen in the first place. We are caught in a deadlock.

The predominance of the logic of capital creates a mental space that is largely hidden from view and bears unforeseen consequences. Its increase leads to violent outbursts of reclaiming profound needs, and the subsequent attempts to fulfill these needs are carried out in often tragic and suicidal ways. We should ask ourselves to what degree the decline of aliveness is related to the emergence of fundamentalism and its associated cruelties. These can be seen in many respects as a distorted way of expressing the need for meaning.

Ecoterrorism, for example, which had long been anticipated as one possible reaction to the global onslaught on life, never really surfaced. But the fact is, it is manifesting itself in many areas; we just don't see the connection, because we don't realize that ecological well-being not only concerns the biosphere, but also our hearts. Rebelling against the decline of this ecology of the heart today is taking on the form of a fundamentalist extortion of fixed order, secure roles, and dogmatic meaning, which are all caricatures of the central experiences of being alive—as being individuals-in-connection.

We are still treating ecological, political, and economical problems with their devastating outcomes as mere technical complications. But in truth they are the result of our forgetfulness about our own aliveness, the consequence of a deep oblivion regarding our real need to be alive. Sadly, and most dangerously, this deep connection is far from obvious. The seeming necessities of the capitalist economy have become the lens through which we view the world. They are accepted as being unchangeable parts of reality, and, in this way, they blind us into not even considering their role in the emergence of global unease and frustration.

I do not want to argue that if we only put aliveness center stage, everything else will align and all our problems will be solved. Again: enlivenment does not propose another utopian solution. Life itself is a paradoxical and problematic phenomenon. It is the dimension of reality in which its inherent incompleteness becomes manifest. We can only deal with this if we focus on an ecological art of living that works on these tensions and imagines them in a meaningful whole, in a material and spiritual commons. This is—as is any participation in an ecosystem—not an unproblematic stance. It is, however, the way our embodied nature yearns to unfold. It is part of the real, which is a mutually fertile ensemble of desiring bodies. To cut ourselves off from that process is to sever life itself: ours, and that of others.

If we hope to make any progress, we must first ask what is blocking us from doing so. We should look for common denominators in our thinking and in our policies that may be responsible so that we can begin to name related problems—and begin to look for a new perspective for facing reality. Then perhaps we can develop a narrative that more accurately describes the world that we live in—and wish to live in. The fact that we have been walking in circles for so long shows, however, that we still don't know—and are not allowed to know—what we truly lack and what we truly need.

BEYOND DEAD MATTER

The central feature of our crisis-ridden civilization is that mainstream thinking takes reality for something it is not. We think it is dead, that we can treat it by means of mechanical rationality. But it is alive. We deny the world's deeply creative, poetic, and expressive processes, all of them constantly unfolding and bringing forth a multitude of fertile, dynamic, and mutually interacting relationships that constitute the biosphere and our own identity. This dismissal is not just an intellectual flaw, but also an emotional one: we usually don't sense these relationships, and we don't sense that we are part of them. They don't have a place in our official descriptions of reality, and they are not granted much space in private awareness. This is more than a conceptual problem: it is an inability to access the actual, feeling self. We may have forgotten what it means to be alive.

But that numbing of our direct experience of reality takes place in an official framework. All of the sciences, whether natural, social, or economic, try to understand the world as if it were a dead, mechanical process that could be examined through statistical or cybernetic analyses. Since Descartes's far-reaching revolution of separating reality into a hidden, subjective, strictly nongeneralizable *res cogitans* on the one hand—our minds—and a visible, malleable, calculable, but dead *res extensa* on the other—the material world—humankind's most noble endeavors have focused on separating reality and all its parts into discrete building blocks: atoms and algorithms. This procedure is still widely regarded as being the most fruitful way to advance human progress.

The scientific rules that are still as valid today as when they were established in the seventeenth century require us to treat everything as dead matter. Occam's razor has become a lethal weapon transforming every object of interest into an assemblage of inanimate building blocks.[6] This tendency has cursed our civilization with the same sort of imprecation that haunted the King Midas. In his insatiable greed, this mythical ruler wished for every object he touched to be turned into gold. The gods eventually fulfilled his desire and the result was that Midas starved to death. Everything that our civilization touches with the X-ray vision of the scientific method in order to understand it and find a useful application for it becomes a resource and in effect loses its aliveness and hence its life-giving ability. Science has erected a metaphysics of the dead in order to block our understanding of the most remarkable aspect of our being in the world, namely, our being alive. Instead of excluding our aliveness, our subjectivity, and the subjectivity of other beings as mere distortions from an "objective" view of the world, we need to incorporate these embodied experiences as instruments of objective perception—objective because this perception is shared between beings.

ENLIGHTENMENT 2.0: ENLIVENMENT

Enlivenment provides a new focus that could help us understand the current global crisis. Enlivenment, as a first approach, means getting things, people, and oneself to live again—to be more full of life, to become more alive. It means considering the world not from the abstract perspective of a functional object, but from the lived perspective of meaningful first-person experience. The idea is at once concerned with the "real life" of threatened species or ecosystems, or people under attack, and with our "inner life" as representatives of the social species *Homo economicus*, who incessantly perform more or less necessary tasks and fulfill more or less real needs to maintain the huge machine we call "the economy."

With the term *enlivenment* we have found a starting point from which to identify the various neglected areas of reality that are hidden in the blind spot of modernist, scientific thinking. It is not accidental that the term bears so much resemblance to the name of its predecessor concept, the *Enlightenment*. With the rise of the Enlightenment, the basic assumptions at the base of modern times became fully dynamic: namely, that the world is understandable on rational grounds; that humans can change it (because we can understand it); and that we not only have the ability but also the right to change it in order to improve the human condition. With the Enlightenment, modern humanism was born, a way of thinking and being that has to an incredible degree improved the living conditions for at least a part of humanity.

But Enlightenment habits of thought—especially the rational and technocratic understanding of human agency—also have a dark side, as famously observed by critics of the "dialectic of Enlightenment."[7] The main flaws of the Enlightenment approach—besides its presumption that reality is essentially transparent on its face and open to all—are its reliance on dualisms of thought, rational discourse, and the

Newtonian subject–object split. As Horkheimer and Adorno (and, in their wake, many others) argue, Enlightenment ideology brought about not only freedom but also some of the great totalitarian-technocratic catastrophes of the twentieth century. This tradition of thought is arguably also responsible for the technocratic disasters of the current unsustainability of our planetary ecosystem.

But critics of the Enlightenment to this day rarely provide a positive alternative concept. They only caution against too much desire for controlling the world in the name of humanism, which in turn amasses even more suspicion against the human character. As any positive image of a human "being" proved to be potentially totalitarian and essentialistic, the critics of the Enlightenment had to become even more suspicious, even stronger advocates of clear analysis and clean separation of humankind from nature, and thus even more fervent proponents of the Enlightenment.

The critics of Enlightenment thinking have in particular elaborated the arbitrariness of our "language games" and the constructedness of all perception, supplanting the Enlightenment's idea of universal humanistic progress through the conquering of nature with a general suspicion against anything "essential," which is to say, fertile and live-giving on its own terms. The sweeping claim of understanding objective reality through human means has been superseded by an attitude of general distrust of anything human, that is, experienced or perceived—particularly one's own feelings—as being "only" subjective and potentially distorted.

The critique of the Enlightenment therefore substituted the totalitarian regime of feasibility with a dictatorship of arbitrary construction and emotional coldness. But these are themselves variations of Enlightenment ideals, and they still dominate the machine dreams of various posthumanist positions.[8] It is this position of radical freedom of the linguistic mind that feeds the Anthropocene idea that all reality is now permeated by human cultural imagination. It supports the claim that we must become "stewards" (actually sovereigns) of reality in order to keep it a livable place for our species. Seen through this lens, we finally hold nature in our hands in its totality, and thus the pledge of Enlightenment is kept at last.

But aliveness is that which desires its own way of transformation before any conscious choice, before any goal is set. It cannot be treated only from the outside, because it is "inside"—as the desire for participation and connection. Therefore, not only human life but also the existence of other beings suffer from the "context of delusion" (Adorno)[9] of universal feasibility. These other beings desire to live as we do. They have no choice but to trust the rightness of their needs. Their feelings answer our own forgotten aliveness through existential gestures. We can make observations of this kind even on the most casual nature walk. Other beings show us a way to the enlightenment of the Enlightenment, which is its enlivenment.

Significantly, the Enlightenment project has no use for the notions of life, sentience, experience, subjectivity, corporeal embodiment, creativity and agency, imagination and poesy. These concepts are not completely excluded from the Enlightenment view of the world, but have been relegated to the powerless private sphere of personal taste and individual consumption. Historically, this separation gave rise to Romanticism, which then faded away in the face of the overpowering success of the sciences and today is viewed mostly as a historical event or a private attitude. The optimism required to mobilize all of reality as a resource on the one hand and the nihilism behind the belief that reality is forever ungraspable on the other thus compound each other. A space devoid of meaning is thereby created that allows for only one winner: the de facto economization of everything for the sake of creating monetary surplus value, which in turn is used to suppress aliveness.

The point in reviewing this familiar history is to stress that Enlightenment norms are not arcane historical or philosophical matters, but deep structural principles in modern culture that have a powerful effect in ordering how we perceive, think, and act. Our economics, legal systems, educational curricula, government policies, and much else are firmly based on Enlightenment principles. Or else they claim to have overcome the principles of the Enlightenment to argue the premises of an extreme dismissal of the Enlightenment, which in essence brings into doubt the coherence of individual embodied experience. These are the reasons why conventional economic and political approaches have been unable to "solve" our sustainability crisis. They reflect profound errors in our understanding of human thought (epistemology), relationships (ontology), and organic functioning (biology).

The idea of enlivenment is meant to be a corrective. It seeks to expand our view of what human beings are as embodied subjects-in-relationship. This notion does not exclude the role of human rationality and agency, but it does connect them with other modes of being, such as our psychological and metabolic relationships with the "more-than-human" world,[10] in both its animate and inanimate aspects. *Enlivenment* links rationality with subjectivity and sentience. It faces the contradictions that arise from this entanglement and builds on them for a new poetic practice of agency.

In doing so, enlivenment positions itself as the true inheritor of the original Enlightenment, which had intended to overcome unjustified dogmas and sought to strengthen the freedom of the subject. Indeed, enlivenment strives to rediscover precisely this freedom—not by excluding the body and its self-organizing nature, but by relying on it as an organ of perception and a creator of values. Enlivenment understands freedom as a dimension of embodied existence, not as a given, but as the constant horizon of a desire to be. Enlivenment attempts to describe this as freedom-in-necessity within a shared biosphere of material, feeling, goal-oriented bodies. The historical Enlightenment strived for emancipation and self-determination of the subject. Enlivenment reclaims for every being the right to expand its own aliveness-in-connection, the right to feel, to see, and to perceive, to be aware of one's own needs, and to stand for the truth of one's own experience, even against dominant trends in thinking.

It is quite possible that the grand political goals the Enlightenment inaugurated two hundred and fifty years ago, and which in many areas of the world are still far from being realized, can be achieved only through a shift to the idea of enlivenment. It might just be possible, for example, that achieving a broader social and economic inclusion in the polity of a state will require a deep "existential recognition" of all citizens in a state, particularly ethnic minorities, which includes each person's genuinely human, even animate, needs, and not just agreed-on minimum material necessities. Universal emancipation may require a deeper understanding—expressed equally in an emotional awareness—of the aliveness of persons in order to grant them the space to accept their needs and to welcome themselves in their own individual identity. The human being as a political being is always an embodied, feeling, and expressive self. For this reason, Enlightenment-style thinking needs to evolve toward the emancipation of our authentic emotional needs in connection with other lives: an Enlightenment 2.0.

WHAT IS LIFE, AND WHAT ROLE DO WE PLAY IN IT?

In using the term *enlivenment* to reorient ourselves in the planetary crisis, we focus on a singular deficiency in contemporary thought: a lack of understanding of what life is. We might even say we have forgotten what life means. We are unaware of our most profound reality as living beings. This absentmindedness is an astonishing fact—but it is also a logical outcome of our rational culture. The "meaning of life" and questions about human purpose, satisfactions, and aspirations have long been ignored in biology, economics, and the humanities—as have our direct, first-person experiences of being a living piece of matter. This anesthesia is the required condition of access to the mainstream fields of biology, economics, and the humanities—and all the more for much of politics, global governance, and economics. The most pressing and most evident question—the purpose of one's existence and that of the other beings—is not seen as part of reality and is given no role in its administration. It is totally private.

And yet, this notion of the "meaning of life" embodies some simple, everyday questions that stand at the center of human experience. It demands that we consider: What do we live for? What are our inner needs as living creatures? What relationships do we have, or should we have, to one another and to the natural order? How do we produce things for our immediate needs? What in fact are these needs? How must we create, maintain, and earn our livelihoods? My proposal is to shift focus to a new question: *What is life, and what role do we play in it?*

It was once considered the highest exercise of human cognition and sentience to explore what life means, to debate which relationships create and maintain it, and to ask how to live it. But for at least the past century, talk about these ancient, crucial dimensions of life have been treated as the dusty relics of some obscure graveyard of intellectual history. It may well be that by excluding such talk about life, its meanings, its dimensions, and the inner tensions between living agents and their relationships, we have lost the most important reference point for acting in a wise and sustainable manner. And we have lost any secure relationship to ourselves. After all, who would deny that he or she is alive?

And yet the existential realities of living are regarded as somehow too prosaic or arcane for discussion. If we are to recover reliable reference points for sustainable living, and in so doing find the wisdom to confront the manifold crises of our time, we must first look for a fresh account of the principles of existence of living beings. This requires that we carefully reconsider how relationships in the biosphere are organized—and experienced—and that we start not by just looking at them from the outside, but by remembering that we are already a feeling part of such relationships. Are there basic rules as to how organisms realize their existence? What makes ecological systems fertile? Which constellations do we experience as fertile? What makes the individual experience of a "full life" possible? How is the metabolism of goods, services, and meaning possible without it degrading the system in which they operate? In the following chapters, I will work through such questions with the goal of formulating the outlines of a culture of life.

These are complicated issues—and yet these are also rather down-to-earth questions. So we should not be afraid of getting too general, or of being too personally involved. Generations of "experts" in different scientific specialties have given in to such fear, paid attention only to technical details, and refused to address the mysteries of lived existence that are shared anew in every moment. The heritage left by such safe, narrow-gauged thinking has been devastating.

I propose a rather pragmatic focus: First, we have to diagnose why we have an aversion to thinking or talking about life. Then, it is important to consider how a contemporary account of life could be imagined without falling back into essentialist thinking, but rather to open genuinely new windows of thought. Finally, we should try to understand what recent scientific findings reveal about the unfolding of life's processes—and how this could lead to a new approach that overcomes a dualist mode of thinking: our reflexive mental habit of separating resources and natural agents, reason and the physical world, human life and animate nature, physical bodies and human meaning.

ENLIVENMENT IS MORE THAN SUSTAINABILITY

If we look back over the last fifty-plus years of sustainability politics, we can note a lot of progress—the enactment of laws to protect nature, the creation of environmental protection agencies, the setting of safety thresholds for toxic materials, the ban on fluorocarbons, and so on. But even with the implied quest for more ecological efficiency the basic contradiction remains: we devour the very biosphere that we are a part of and that we depend upon. From this perspective, we have not been able to get any closer to solving the sustainability question; we remain trapped in its underlying, fundamental contradictions.

The different view of sustainability I will develop in this essay, therefore, does not emphasize technical improvement or sound treatment of scarce resources as a priority. Rather, it sees in the goal of "leading a fuller life" the most important stepping-stone toward changing our relationships with the animate Earth and with ourselves. From this standpoint, it is easy to see that there is indeed a connection between the idea of sustainability and the condition of the individual self, as well as an antiproportional relation between rising efficiency and individually increasing stress (although neoliberalism denies this). If we adopt this perspective, we will begin to see that something is sustainable if it enables more life—for myself, for other human individuals involved, for the ecosystem, and for the culture as a whole. It is crucial to rediscover the link between our inner experience and the "external" natural order. Reclaiming the right to feel our needs authentically as embodied beings needing connection can then become the primary political act.

To understand what "more aliveness" means from the standpoint of sustainability, and to help us put the human species and the rest of nature on the same plane, I propose that we regard "our communal life as embodied beings" as a common denominator for all living organisms. We know this dimension since we inhabit the world from the inside, as subjective beings. At the same time, it is a category that binds together individual lives and defines life as a reciprocal process. Life is what we all share. And life is what we all can feel. The emotional experience of feeling our needs and having them satisfied is a direct sign of how well we realize (or fail to realize) our aliveness. This is valid for humans, but equally so for all other animals: for fungi, plants, bacteria, archaea—indeed, for all cellular life.

The world is a place that constantly seeks to express its creative powers through a continuous interplay of meaningful relationships. In this scenario of "life as embodied beings," human beings, as natural creatures, experience the forces and structures of nature as much as other beings do. But we humans have our species-specific way of dealing with the openness of nature and the unfolding natural history of freedom. We are able to access a symbolic culture through which we imagine a practice that provides the basic elements of fertile aliveness according to particular needs, ideas, and places, so that the propagation of fertile aliveness becomes a constant overtone to any imaginative practice.[11]

If we understand sustainability as aliveness and therefore as that which makes us vibrant with means for personal growth and development, it gives us an entirely new (and more accurate) field of vision for understanding the challenges we must meet. As Storm Cunningham once put it: Nobody will be very impressed if you answer the question "How is your marriage?" with "Oh, it's sustainable." But everyone would be filled with envy if you replied: "Well, it's energizing. It makes me feel alive."[12] From the experience of aliveness (which is always to a certain degree lived and felt in the first person), we can decide many questions as to what the most sustainable action might be: it is that which gives the most life, that which is most fertile.

ENLIVENMENT AND THE GREEN NEW DEAL

From an Anthropocene standpoint, the dualism of the Enlightenment has come to an end. This has immediate consequences for our habitual regard for nature as a wholesome other in need of protection. Some thinkers propagating a coming "age of man" go so far as to accuse ecologists of a romantic fixation with a health-giving nature, and to see in that the biggest obstacle to an efficient safeguarding of species and ecosystems.

The standard ecological program for the Anthropocene no longer wishes to exclude nature from human activities as something foreign and fragile, but hopes to protect other beings through these activities. This stance is gaining increasing prominence on green agendas. The benefits are thought to go in both directions: ecosystem services are meant to provide economic benefits, while at the same time the ecosystems and organisms providing these services are supposed to be protected through their increased market value. "Ecological economics" means integrating natural processes in our economic system and putting a virtual price tag on their performances.[13]

The Anthropocene position shares with this notion of a green economy the underlying anthropocentric assumption—that we can (or even must) start from a uniquely human standpoint if we are to come to terms with the problems of sustainability. Both regard Darwinistic theories and free-market ideology as the inexorable premises of economic life. Another difference between both anthropocentric approaches and the enlivenment idea is their stance on perfectibility. Many Anthropocene thinkers are strictly utopian in believing that technology can optimize imperfect nature; the biocentrism of the enlivenment perspective recognizes, as a matter of theory, the unavoidable messes, shortcomings, and drains on efficiency that are part of biological and human reality, which no cultural or technological improvements can overcome.

The idea behind enlivenment differs fundamentally from those popular, faddish proposals for designing a "green economy" as a transition toward a "green new deal."[14] In these proposals, the dualist opposition between human culture and nature and its resources is not even addressed, let alone resolved. If anything, these policy approaches intensify this dualist tension by trying to increase technological efficiency and the objectification of nature.

The "green new deal" and related positions agree that nature also behaves according to the features of economically feasible human behavior, such as efficiency, parsimony, selection, and constant innovation. They are convinced that these presumably natural principles can be used for a revolution in efficiency. We will see in the next chapter that an argument about nature that in reality is derived from human cultural prejudices will not yield the desired outcome in terms of sustainability and fairness.

Philosophically, this argument is a *petitio principii*. It posits the observed outcome as the underlying reason for that outcome. Ecologically, it is not in line with what happens in living systems. All forms of green economy are marked by the idea that nature is a market with flows of goods and services. This standpoint leads less to an appreciation of the value of natural processes than to the integration of these processes into the production logics of the market economy. It sacrifices aliveness in favor of a higher demand for efficiency. This is the exploitation of life's powers that are freely given and thus follows a very old schematic.

In this essay, I shall not criticize the "green economy" approach on the basis of its capacity or inability to incite real change. Let me just say here that the potential of the green economy to reverse things is at least doubtful. Critics point to the "rebound effect" (or the Jevons paradox), in which increased efficiencies from green innovation may decrease the resources used in a given market and accordingly lower the costs invested for using that resource, but they also free up that money to spend on other things, resulting in massive net increases in economic growth and resource usage. We can see this effect at work in the increased carbon dioxide production caused by "efficient" information technologies and the Internet.

But the much bigger problem is this: all proposed "efficiency revolutions" invariably point to nature itself as the supreme model of *effectiveness*—not of aliveness. But this model is wrong. Nature is not efficient. It is wasteful, sloppy, forgetful, dreamy, without plan—and in all this it is highly redundant. This boils down to one thing: nature's products and agents (including us) are to a huge extent edible. This is the term for "fully recyclable" from an enlivenment perspective. We can see that it brings with it notions of communion and transformation, fear and antagonism, materiality and emotion. The web of life cannot be thought or mended without these.

Living beings make up one interrelated, embodied whole, and humans comprise only a fractional portion of this whole. The real flaw of the efficiency approach to sustainability is that nature is still seen as something "outside" us that can be used for human means. But nature is not outside us. It is inside us—and we are inside it.

There is a limit to any increase in efficiency, and that limit is the natural imperfection of embodied being—the "necessary imperfection of every creation," as the previously cited Gershom Scholem called it. Humans as natural beings will always suffer from the deficiencies of this imperfect state and enjoy its gifts. It is the imperfection of any conceivable reality. Its inhabitants are mortal and full of contradictions—as is every organism. Higher efficiency is not capable of improving on that. But it can veil this basic structure, which offers tragedy and bliss, and it can seduce us into thinking up simple solutions, in which we blind ourselves into forgetting that we cannot only take, we must also give. Efficiency as a solution in order to pay justice to reality amounts to a "category error" in thinking.

The enlivenment idea differs from the green economy approach in another key respect: whereas green economy remains committed to the idea of material "growth" as the best way to improve the conditions of life, an enlivenment position recognizes that nature does not grow in absolute terms. The "GDP of the biosphere" (if one may be so absurd) has remained constant for a very long time. Ecology is a steady-state economy. It does not grow; it evolves. The only factor of nature that expands is its immaterial dimension, which could be called a *depth of experience*: the diversity of natural forms and the variety of ways to experience aliveness.

A SCIENCE FOR LIFE

The refusal to study aliveness as a scientific phenomenon, however, is lessening. Today many scientific disciplines that have long rejected a worldview that could open up space for the primordial human experience of embodied feeling have begun to search for a way out of the impasse. They acknowledge aliveness as the pivotal point of a future human self-understanding. Independent of each other, such disciplines as biology, psychology, physics, and even economics are rediscovering the phenomenon of living.

Biology in particular is learning that sentience and felt expression in organisms are not just epiphenomena but rather the way living beings exist in the first place. Biologists are working in exciting times, as huge changes to their scientific paradigm are happening. The ground is well prepared. Scientists like the Harvard-based embryologists Marc Kirschner and John Gerhart, the Copenhagen and Tartu-based theoretical biologists Jesper Hoffmeyer and Kalevi Kull, and science theoretician Evelyn Fox Keller have started to acknowledge that meaning and expressiveness are deeply rooted in the heart of nature. Such eminent biological thinkers as Lynn Margulis, Francisco Varela,

Terrence Deacon, Stuart Kauffman, and Gregory Bateson have opened up a picture in which organisms are seen no longer as machines competing with other machines but rather as a focus of existential self-interest, which not only exist in a material way but are also continuously making and expressing experiences.

Being alive, these researchers wish to show, is not a case of mere cause and effect, but also involves the play of embodied interest and hence experiences and feelings. Brain researchers like Antonio Damasio have shown that these emotions, not abstract cognition, are the stuff of mind. The findings of ecopsychology make clear that if we can freely relate to other beings in a more-than-human world, we have more space to unfold our identities as humans: we feel healthier and succinctly more "ourselves."[15]

If we consider all this current change in biology, a completely different picture of the living world emerges, one in which humans no longer stand outside, but are deeply woven into material, mental, and emotional exchange processes with the rest of life. This new vision has the potential to lead to the sort of major paradigm change that happened in physics in the early 1900s.

Physical science for a long time now has been able to show that the separation of an observer (subject) and an observed phenomenon (object) is an artifact of causal-mechanic, linear thought. For quantum physics, there is no locality or temporal chronology. Rather, any event can be connected to any other. The physicist David Bohm has called this the "implicate order" of the cosmos. This view not only calls into question locality and chronology, it blurs the separation of physical and psychological reality. We exist in a space-time that is a continuum of "insides" (meanings) and "outsides" (bodies)—not in an empty space filled with objects, but as part of a matrix of relations and their meanings.[16]

Biology is heading for a turn similar to the one physics took a hundred years ago. It has set out to explore the emotional, symbolic, and metabolic connection of the human observer with the rest of the biosphere. Each scientific witness of the biological world—who is as much an organism as the one being researched—is not only a spectator, but at the same time his or her own subject of research, being made of the same stuff, and experiencing aliveness from within. One of the first renowned biological scientists who recently changed his attitude to admit a dimension of irreducible inwardness in his concept of the human organism is the evolutionary scientist E. O. Wilson. Wilson has distanced himself from the idea of the "egoistic gene" of his colleague Richard Dawkins. For Dawkins, experience, subjectivity, and culture are illusions that only serve the successful passing on of one's genes to the next generation. Wilson in turn defended the density of the cultural imagination as something that ultimately cannot be objectified, as it brings existential answers to the complexity and contradictoriness of our biological reality. In order to explore this opening of biological thinking to biological subjectivity, Wilson thinks nothing less than a "second enlightenment" will be necessary.[17]

If natural processes inevitably give way to subjectivity, meaning, and feeling, our science, and our science-based policy and economy, must take these lived dimensions into account. This second Enlightenment is a new stage of cultural evolution that can safeguard our scientific (and democratic) ideals of common access to knowledge and the powers connected with it, while at the same time validating personal experience that is felt and subjective and therefore the defining essence of embodied experience. The enlivenment I envision includes other animate beings, which, after all, share the same capacities for embodied experiences and "world-making."

The multifaceted farewell to the cliché of objectivity also has consequences for another crucial area where ideas of exchange and communion are forged: the economy. Economic activity is about more than the give-and-take of goods or money. It in fact consists of a broad palette of material flows and meaningful relationships. This multilayered dimension in which material and symbolic-emotional aspects are intertwined is being rediscovered by a quickly growing revolutionary branch of economy: commons theory.

Commons thinking takes seriously the metaphor of householding and puts the proper task of the economy—the sensible allocation and fair distribution of resources—back in the center of biospheric husbandry. For commons thinking, economic processes consist of flows of matter and relations in an ecosystem. These don't just center on goods, but also create lived meaning. Allocation and sense-making are inseparable.

Whether they realize it or not, humans engage in the ecological exchange of gifts, which not only distributes material goods and services but also creates a sense of belonging and dedication, and hence feeling and meaning. In any habitat, the ecological exchange comprises a flowing back and forth of matter, energy, and existential related-ness in an economy of "natural gifts."[18] Seen from this view-point, economic exchange cannot meaningfully distinguish between agents and resources as wholly independent enti-ties; they are entangled with each other. Life can never be just a resource; it is always also a gift received by the other members of the ecosystem whose contributions are neces-sary for a living subject to survive.

Metabolic exchange is always meaningful. It is a poetic revelation of the whole through particular transactions. This meaning is conveyed as a gift. We can learn more about that hidden dimension in all economic exchange through a field that may at first seem unrelated to it: art. As ecological exis-tence is possible only through gifts, so, as Lewis Hyde observes, is art. This has to do with the fact that art tries to capture aliveness from the inside. For the living self to be revealed in a work of art, a fundamental dimension of its ecological relatedness must appear in the nature of the work as gift.

This brings me to the last dimension in which the notion of aliveness is increasingly gaining ground: artistic expres-sion, artistic work, and artistic research. Artworks never try to demonstrate content in purely objective terms, but always allow for an experience of at least partial entanglement. Creative processes do not represent the world but let it come alive in a symbolic way by being contagious to the observer with the kind of experience they intend to convey. Artistic expression and poetic experience are the cultural reservoir from which we can learn about aliveness from the inside and start our own explorations of it, even though art's own self-understanding sometimes misses that perspective or rejects it.

Artists—like ecosystems—work with the imagination and know that it is a real force that can incite productive transformations. Intensified aliveness always amounts to greater self-expression and deepened poetic experience. Consequently, any change meant to pay justice to the human (and hence lived) dimension can take hold only if it becomes an artistic process. Each artistic act is an act of aliveness. It cannot be demonstrated or represented; it can only be shared.[19]

The new picture of reality that the arts and sciences promise is one of a deeply sentient and meaningful universe. Reality is *poetic*—productive of new life forms and ever-new embodied experiences. It is expressive of all the subjective experiences that individuals undergo. It is a universe in which human subjects are no longer separated from other organisms but instead form a mesh of existential relationships—a quite real "web of life." This "flesh of the world," as the French philosopher Merleau-Ponty called it, is perhaps best understood as a creative game of overcoming unsolvable paradoxes from moment to moment, no matter the realm—ecology, culture, economics, or the arts.[20] The "flesh of the world" is a desire for touch and connection manifesting itself in living gestures of aliveness.

Seen from this perspective, any policy for fostering sustainability acquires a new scope and a new metrics of success. Sustainability can be successful only if it enhances the aliveness of human agents, and of nature and society. It will thus be enriching to develop a more deliberate *enlivened policy*—not as a matter of natural laws dictating the order of human society, but as a strategy to honor the manifold embodied needs of sentient individuals in a more-than-human world.

Sustainable actions from an enlivenment perspective would be actions that over the long run make the continuity of life processes possible. Sustainability is not just about ensuring the simple replenishment of supply; it is about generating more life, creating new possibilities of development, and meeting needs in novel ways. The economist Manfred Max-Neef has shown that basic needs are nonhierarchical and that neglecting even one of them can have pathological consequences.[21] Hence, "more life" cannot be defined in either material or psychological terms. It means a life that produces more meaning and participatory experience, and even more beauty. A full life is a beautiful life—although it can also be a difficult, even tragic life.

A NEW NARRATIVE OF LIVING RELATIONSHIPS

It is necessary to explore a new narrative for what life is, what it is to be alive, what living systems do, and what their goals are. We need to explore how values are created by the realization of the living, and how we, as living beings in a living biosphere, can adapt to that reality, the only reality we have. The new narrative needed cannot be a "talking about" the other as if of something unrelated and alien. It cannot be a sequence of answers, as we have not even figured out the questions. The needed narrative can be nothing other than a form of *talking*. This talking is also a dialogue with those remote areas in ourselves that are reflexively silenced by our fear of rocking the boat, of not being in accord with the dominant paradigm. We need to ask ourselves how life brings forth meaningful experiences and existential values through its realization and how we can imagine the necessary metabolism with the rest of the biosphere out of the scope of this reality—the only reality we have at our disposal.

Even though this narrative will encompass different areas and disciplines, life is the binding dimension for all of them. As a living being, the human organism integrates and connects diverse fields of existential experience, metabolic exchange, and social relationships. The narrative that I propose is by no means an objectivist account, however—it is no mechanics or cybernetics of reality. It will be objective in the sense that poetics is objective: transmitting shared feelings by working in the open dimension of continuous imagination, which is the field of life itself. The narrative that I wish to unfold here will thus strive for "poetic objectivity" or "poetic precision." This is the appropriate way to describe the living world with its endless unfolding of existential relationships and meanings.

Nature, from the enlivening perspective, is not a causal-mechanic object but a relational network of subjects who have individual interests in staying alive, growing, and unfolding. Thus, enlivenment means pushing biological thinking beyond the paradigm shift physics underwent a hundred years ago and which led to the end of Newtonian thinking. To end Newtonian thinking concerning the biosphere—other organisms, ourselves as embodied beings, and the whole of ecological and economical exchange processes—will mean acknowledging that we, the human observers, are as alive and expressive as the organisms and ecosystems we observe. Such a biology is emphatically nonreductionist. Its main goal is to understand how freedom is anchored in a material, living world.

Enlivenment, therefore, is not another naturalist description of ourselves and our world intended only to translate our findings into whatever specific policies or economics are needed. The reflection I propose is indeed naturalist—but it offers a naturalism that is based on the idea of nature as an unfolding practice of ever-growing freedom and creativity paradoxically linked to material and embodied processes. The biosphere is alive in the sense that it not only obeys the rules of deterministic or stochastic interactions of particles, molecules, atoms, fields, and waves. The biosphere is also about producing agency, expression, and meaning.

Once we start appreciating reality as a living process, everything changes. This is the challenge posed by enlivenment as a paradigm for the transition to a new way of thinking that encompasses feeling and acting at the same time. If we put the lived truth that is shared with others at center stage, it provides a strong ethical mandate to intervene in our global system. Enlivenment not only suggests strategies of change, but shifts the perspective under which any change is experienced. It offers an invitation to participate in life.

2 BIOECONOMICS: THE HIDDEN MEGASCIENCE

Two doctrines rule our times. One is Neo-Darwinism, with its tenet of biological optimization, in which functional adaptations supposedly create biodiversity. The other is neoliberalism, with its concept of economic efficiency, supposedly creating wealth and equal distribution. There is an astonishing interconnection and a huge mutual support between these two guiding metaphysics of our culture.

For more than a hundred and fifty years, both assumptions have become intertwined streams of one coherent pattern of thought that forms the basic matrix of our official understanding of reality. They form the "BIOS (basic input/output system)" of our ontology. The same way that the BIOS in a PC is inaccessible to the user interface but still determines how the operating system communicates with the hardware, the BIOS of our culture is very difficult to question, as even critical queries are still formulated in a language mirroring the implicit ontological assumptions.

The BIOS defines what can be talked about in the first place. Everything else must remain in the mist of vague personal notions and is very difficult to incorporate into a culture's self-understanding. Efficient optimization is the "absolute metaphor" of our age, in the sense that the German cultural philosopher Hans Blumenberg used the term to understand how certain cultural concepts create reality. There is no deeper cognitive foundation than these concepts. They are the material from which our worldview is built. Nonetheless, they can be wrong.[1]

The premises of Neo-Darwinism and neoliberalism constitute the prevailing tacit understanding of how the world works. Inside their deep and compact logical structure, the two currents of biological and economic optimization theory are so mutually reinforcing and normative that respectable thought considers them to be beyond question.[2] It is not by chance that "*eco*-nomy" and "*eco*-logy" are nearly identical terms. Both build on the metaphor of housekeeping and the provisioning of existential goods and services (the Greek word *oikos* means "house," "householding," or "family"). Both describe the organization of existential supply, the provisioning of essential goods and services, which in both cases is organized in very similar ways.

Ecology, like economy, starts from the idea that keeping a house and making a living is a theater of competition and contest whose object is ever-more optimal efficiency. Survival means defeating others, and greater efficiency is necessary if one is to outsmart one's adversary. In the Neo-Darwinian, neoliberal narrative, the household is not, however, a place where feeling agents pursue their individual good. On this view, the household does not mean home and a warm hearth. The householding process is strangely conceived of as being completely subjectless. Its logic does not take account of the actual presence of agents, let alone their needs. Indeed, it does not take life into account at all.

In their current dominant forms, both ecology and economy conceive of the process of householding as subjectless and self-organized in the sense that eternal, external laws (of selection and of the free market) reward or punish the behavior of the more or less fit elements—atomistic black boxes called *Homo economicus*—economic man—or in its more modern formulation, the "selfish gene." To yield results in this framework of thinking, neither contemporary economics nor "ecosciences" need to consider actual, lived experience. The agenda has excluded life in the existential, experiential sense. The prevailing bioeconomic megascience provides the deep metaphysics of our age. It is a science of nonliving.

EFFICIENCY METAPHYSICS AS NINETEENTH-CENTURY SOCIAL REALITY

Both Darwinism and liberalism were born in pre-Victorian England at about the same time. Their theoretical premises explicitly and inexplicitly refer to the social conditions and practices of a country that had been undergoing the wrenching disruptions of industrialization. At that time there existed a rigidly stratified society without any structured system of social care and cooperation.

This situation delivered the framework for a cultural climate that gave birth to both evolutionary theory and modern economic thinking, each one providing inspiration to the other. We can probably even say that, fundamentally, both "eco-" theories are branches of the same encompassing ontological framework. Ecology and economy, with their focus on material competition and the selection of optimally functioning objects, are built on the same underlying doctrine. Through their intellectual proximity to each other, Darwinian evolutionary thinking and Adam Smith's free-market theories became a sort of political economy of nature.

While Charles Darwin was struggling to provide an explanation for the diversity of living nature, political economist Thomas Robert Malthus proposed an idea that would become pivotal in the development of evolutionary theory and today's understanding of biology as being the result of evolution-by-optimization. Malthus was obsessed with the idea of scarcity as a driving force of social change. There will never be enough resources to feed a population that steadily multiplies, he argued, and a struggle for dominance must take place in which the weakest will necessarily lose.

Charles Darwin adopted this piece of socioeconomic theory, drawn from Malthus's observations of Victorian industrial society, and applied it to his own comprehensive theory of natural change and development. Darwin could not have developed his empirical-biological theory of selection through his discoveries on the voyage on the *Beagle* alone, but had to have been informed by something beyond observations of real long-term natural change. The father of evolutionary theory needed to incorporate ideas derived from the social practices of his time. Apart from drawing on Malthus for the idea of a natural overproduction of offspring in order to allow selection its forming powers, Darwin's argument relied on the experiences and practices of Victorian breeders. At that point in time, these experiences and practices were creating the modern concept of biological "race" as a sum of optimal qualities developed for a certain task needed to be more economically successful. Darwin himself was a breeder and raised pigeons and orchids, among other species.

The resulting discipline, evolutionary biology, is a more accurate reflection of pre-Victorian social practices than of natural reality. In the wake of this metaphorical takeover, such concepts as the *struggle for existence*, *competition*, *growth*, and *optimization*—which were central justifications for the political status quo in pre-Victorian England—tacitly became centerpieces of our own self-understanding as embodied and social beings. And they remain so today— especially in those parts of the world that still resemble parts of pre-Victorian England in their social organizations.

Biological, technological, and social progress, so the argument goes, is brought forth by the sum of individual egos (egoistical genes or utility-maximizing agents) striving to outcompete each other. In a perennial contest, fit species (powerful corporations) exploit niches (markets) and multiply their survival rate (profit margins), whereas weaker (less efficient) ones go extinct (bankrupt). This double metaphysics of economics and nature, however, reveals far more of our society's opinion about itself than it offers any objective account of the biological world.

In fact, the amalgamation of ecology and economy is explicitly directed against the idea of understanding reality as a commons. It is a bulwark against experiencing life as an interrelatedness of ecosystems that can be brought to flower through a culture of exchange and mutual enabling.

Malthus developed his theory around the climax of the enclosure movement. At that time, the urban population was growing rapidly: peasants were still being driven from their rural villages to the cities by land owners who had taken the commons away from common use and started to intensify agriculture through private enterprise. Here the concept of the efficient breed overlapped with the idea of efficient land use. Both turned life into a mere resource, something to compete for with others.

The historical process through which private landowners had excluded the human population from the ecosystem that sustained its livelihood was something Malthus regarded not as a social but as a natural effect.[3] To Malthus, it seemed obvious that there were not enough resources to feed everybody, but in reality these resources had been taken away by some. This is another case of *petitio principii*, of taking a consequence to be the cause of a problem and accordingly regarding the victims of these consequences as being their ostensible source. This style of toxic reasoning is part and parcel of the attempts of liberal economics to enforce allegedly necessary measures that destroy processes of aliveness.

The reciprocal borrowing of metaphors between the disciplines not only transformed biology. It also mirrored back onto economics, which came to see itself more and more as a "hard" natural science. Economics deliberately derived its models from biology and physics, culminating in the formulation of the mathematical concept of *Homo economicus*. University textbooks still invoke nineteenth-century economists who mingled concepts from the natural sciences with economic theory. The British economist and logician William Jevons postulated that economics should describe human relationships in all of their aspects and consequently formulate the laws of the heart. His French colleague Léon Walras claimed that "economic equilibrium" follows deterministic laws imported from physics.[4]

The resulting picture—the individual as a machine-like egoist always seeking to maximize his utility—has become the implicit but all-influencing model of human values and behavior. It has cast its shadow over an entire generation of psychological and game-theoretical approaches to economics. For its part, evolutionary biology has also taken inspiration from economic models. The idea of the "selfish gene," for example, is not much more than the metaphor of *Homo economicus* extended to biochemistry.

It should not be surprising, then, that biology and economics have come to function as two branches of one science. Each works with the same structural assumptions as the other. And both exclude the sphere of living beings and lived experience from their description of reality. The great danger of this closed, totalistic pattern of thinking is its capacity to obscure reality and become a self-fulfilling prophecy. If we are convinced that we have to describe reality as nonliving and treat it accordingly, life and living processes become highly problematic fields of thought and action. They become inscrutable, if not suspect. They die.

This is our predicament today. If our formal systems of thought about the biosphere describe it as nonliving, violence against aliveness will be the outcome. If we conceive of human beings as *Homo economicus*, as nonsentient automatons whose behaviors can be described by algorithms, sentience will be ignored, if not forbidden, and felt experience will be seen as irrelevant. A bioeconomical ontology will inevitably generate an indifference toward life, which will lead to both a loss of species and an extinction of experience. It will result in anesthesia toward lived experience and emotional needs.

To see reality as a living process, on the other hand, changes everything. Such is the challenge offered by the transcendent paradigm of enlivenment. Its insistence that our policies focus on lived experience provides the deepest possible ethical leverage for intervening in our global system.[5] Such an approach is moot in today's political culture, of course. But political change must start with our imagining a different reality. Only by imagining a different world have people ever been able to change the current one.

ENCLOSURE OF THE SOUL

We can call the alliance between biology and economics an *economic ideology of nature*. Today it reigns supreme over our understanding of human culture and the world. It defines our embodied dimension (*Homo sapiens* as a gene-governed survival machine) as well as our social identity (*Homo economicus* as an egoistic maximizer of utility). The idea of universal competition unifies the natural and the socioeconomic spheres. It validates the notion of rivalry and predatory self-interest as inexorable facts of life. You have to eliminate as many competitors as possible and take the biggest piece of cake for yourself. The economic ideology of nature amounts to a license to steal life from others.

In truth, the roots of this thinking precede pre-Victorianism. The philosopher Thomas Hobbes famously viewed the world as a "war of all against all." But this was also an echo of the contemporary culture—not an observation based on any absolute, eternal reality. Hobbes lived in a time that saw the forcible enclosure of the commons—the private theft of nature's abundant supplies, which had previously been open in principle to everyone.

This process is described as the *enclosure of the commons*. Starting in the sixteenth century in Britain, it had its most intense period in the late 1700s and early 1800s. By 1830 the privatization of British land was mostly complete and the last medieval structures had been broken down. In other European countries it took considerably longer and has never become entirely completed. In Germany, the first enclosures led to the brutal peasant wars of the sixteenth century. In Britain, entire villages were shut down and their populations deported to the North American or Australian colonies. Everywhere, enclosures resulted in an impoverished rural population feeding into the destitute lower classes in the growing cities, which then became the recruitment pool of workers for budding industry.

The colonization of the non-European world in many places was a high-speed enclosure of fertile and beautifully functioning commons. The Native American world, for example, had been built on the principles of mutual giving and reciprocity with humans and other beings. When the colonialists arrived, this cosmos was literally overrun and nearly destroyed.

The theft of the commons was not just a political process. With it also began the enclosure of consciousness—a control over legitimate existential and emotional needs, and a rule over that which could be considered as really existing as opposed to merely imagined. In his influential book *The Great Transformation*, the economist Karl Polanyi described how economic rationality took over the practice of participating in the ecosystem. This "great transformation" destroyed the understanding that humans are part of a wider community of the living. It led to a world in which there is nothing but merchandise: humans, sold as work force, and nature, sold as resource.

In his legendary analysis, Polanyi explained that the rise of fascism and Stalinism were explosive counter-reactions to the enclosure of aliveness that operated through economical restraints. It is sobering that the control of the market economy today is even stronger than it was in the 1920s. What was then the "Gold Standard" of banking is today the rule of the International Monetary Fund. From here we can gain a fresh—and startling—perspective on the rise of neo-fascism, be it in the form of religious extremism or post-democratic populism.[6]

The enclosure and the contemporary economy that came in that enclosure's wake and separated it into resources and consumers, cause and effect, and nothing else, not only governed the allocation of land, but also redistributed the spaces of our consciousness. In reality, the forced separation between that which gave life (the biosphere) and those who were gifted by life (the commoners) was an act of violence on the part of the landlord, who excluded members of the ecosystem from their rightful positions and thereby damaged these participants, the ecosystem itself, and the unifying experience of self-organizing coherence. The landlord did so, though, through the power of modern science, which provided the necessary conceptual apparatus for going about it.

The declaration of the domination of nature—expressed famously by Francis Bacon—was less an insight into how reality works than a strategy to conquer, devised by the ruling class of a highly hierarchical society averse to all forms of sharing. The unfolding of modern economic thinking with its focus on endless competition has developed in tandem with dualism. Could we even say that dualism is itself capitalism? The metaphysical division of the world into "brute matter" to be exploited and "human culture" to exploit it permanently casts human livelihood in a problematic—even absurd—relationship with the rest of the universe. But it also automatically withdraws existential rights from all those who live in a deeper reciprocity with that universe.

This regime has reigned until today. It encloses our minds and prohibits certain thoughts. It works through a *Denkverbot*, as the lawful canceling out of others' thoughts is called in German. Among such current thought prohibitions is the claim that emotions—although they build the fundamental structure of our experience—can play no role in any valid description of reality. But prohibitions of thoughts—or feelings—have had practical consequences. To the degree that we do not allow ourselves to think as selves-in-connection, we lock ourselves out of nature, we distance our soul from it. You might call the ensuing state what Heidegger described as a "metaphysical homeless-ness." The colonists who originally enclosed physical stretches of land to use them in a more profitable way were as poor metaphysically as the colonized they drove away were poor materially. This is what happens when we break the chain of gifts, even if it is seemingly in our own favor: everyone becomes poorer.

The ideologies of mercilessness that followed the physical enclosures are symptoms of this situation. Through the power of a few mighty proprietors, humanity was expelled from the cosmos in which it had played an active role and which had nourished it. Through their material possessions, the landowners also controlled the narrative. Contrary to what Antonio Gramsci claimed, cultural hegemony followed wealth. These few wealthy powerful subjects exiled human-kind from our surrounding nature, which had supplied us with connectedness and an experience of being connected to reality. Now other beings could no longer be related to in simple terms, but came to be viewed as enemies, inhabiting a "nature red in tooth and claw." What had been a place of connectedness became, through the interests of power on the part of a few agents, responsible for the misery that in truth was not caused by "cruel nature," but was something inflicted by pitiless human suppressors. A near-perfect crime. Psychologists call such kinds of conflation *projection*. What had been the moving force of a few actors, egoism without reciprocity, was transformed into a characteristic of the domain being suppressed in order to scapegoat it. This way of twisting reality is part and parcel of any toxic relationship with a deeply disturbed individual. No genuine relationship can be built in such an atmosphere.

Economical thinking supplies the tools to acquire physically what culture had already conceptually colonized as "raw matter." Culture, dominated by wealthy owners, holds a monopoly on ascribing meaning. In many respects, it was this move that created the major problems of philosophy that continue to occupy us today—such as Kant's question of how experience of the external world is possible. The agony of separation which has made so many thinkers suffer, and which has been an urgent topic for philosophical thought since British and German Romanticism, is at least in part a product of this ideology of separation, which was built not on conceptual grounds but on the very real self-interest of very real actors.

One could even argue that the ecological problem is at root a problem of equality—and that democracy needs a healthy connection to the proper aliveness of its participants if it is not to be overrun by mental colonization. We will see in more detail below to what degree this connection was realized in the social organizations of Stone Age societies. Original indigenous societies are nearly always without a sovereign. Decisions are carried out by a chosen committee, which can be dissolved at any time. Democracy could gain a lot more support in societies if full reciprocity were to become the standard of all relationships. Reciprocity on every level of exchange means not only understanding exchange as a social practice granting emotional identity from the very start, but grasping the fact that breathing and eating, loving and caring, are also forms of exchange. Social as well as ecological problems immediately kick in when the idea of reciprocity as a cosmic principle is violated and stops guiding human actions, something that arguably happened with the transition of hunter-gatherer societies to agricultural societies.[7]

It is noteworthy that, contrary to many philosophers who tackle the dualistic setup as if it were an objective dilemma, some liberal economists openly acknowledge the inadequacy of their worldview even as they cling to it obsessively. John Maynard Keynes, for example, criticized the standard framework of economic thinking as something that perverted life's most noble attitudes. "For at least another hundred years, we must pretend to ourselves and to everyone that fair is foul and foul is fair; for foul is useful and fair is not," he wrote.[8] But Keynes also believed in the usefulness of dividing the world in two, in order to prevent it from sliding into the abyss. Keynes was also invested in a toxic relation to reality: "Avarice and usury and precaution must be our gods for a little longer still," he proclaimed, if we are to proceed from "economic darkness into daylight." Few have delivered a more accurate description of the pact with the Devil.

DUALISM AS COLONIZATION

Dualism, therefore, is not a mere abstraction.[9] It has been the driving force separating humans from the experience of creative vitality. It lies at the heart of the historical Enlightenment idea that the world can become a habitable place only by means of reason. Applying reason to the world means systematically arranging its building blocks in a setting that is completely independent of the actions of a reasoning agent. Reason is also the basis for the logic of the market that differentiates between actors and things. All of these phenomena are consequences of an enclosure that is initially imaginary, but then becomes performative. Like a self-fulfilling prophecy, dualism leads to a material split in reality, to a wounded world. The liberal market system, which makes a distinction between resources (which are traded) and subjects (who trade or who want to be supplied with things), is the product of this conceptual dualism.

From this perspective, there is no difference between enclosure, commodification, and colonization. All three movements attack living systems that have no human owner but are owned only by themselves, as is the case with everything that is truly alive and life-giving. At the same time, they trample on the psychological and emotional identities connected to these resources, because ignoring the fact that beings are life-giving kills them off. Colonization in any form is an attack on aliveness itself as it denies a capacity of life that is unavailable and incomprehensible to the dualistic mind. It is therefore also an attack on reality. Political scientist David Johns observes: "Colonialism is nowhere more apparent and thriving than in the relationship between humanity and the rest of the earth."[10]

We can probably say that capitalism is in reality just that: a predatory takeover of aliveness that thrives on the self-creating powers of beings and exploits their unquench-able desire to give life. It is no wonder, then, that capitalism exploits the "resources" of nature, of the family, of females (as caretakers for and givers of life). Capitalism must use up the gifts of life of others because it is supremely unproduc-tive. To be fertile is to be life-giving. Capitalism, however, is the systematic denial of the principle of the gift, and it draws its energy from this denial. It ultimately feeds on our capac-ity to give life. Living beings cannot help but offer this gift, because life is built on the principle of giving oneself away in order to transform.

The resources capitalism can exploit are therefore close to endless. They will only cease to flow with the actual death of the aliveness it has subjugated: with the literal break-down of nature, fertile relationships, and families. The claim that capitalism creates surplus value by means of the actions of capital is wrong. It reduces the gift of life to noth-ing but monetary wealth, and only for the relatively few in charge. The true work of capitalism has been so well hidden until today because, although natural systems are being overtaxed and the number of species is in sharp decline, the gift of life remains only relatively scarce. This means two things: first, life in the biosphere is still abundantly fertile and productive, and second, life will go on wasting itself abundantly until its last string breaks, leaving an imminent catastrophe hidden. True scarcity is invisible because life will go on giving its gift away until its last breath, for such is its nature. Capitalism's stratagem produces the nearly per-fect crime. Its traces are invisible because of the victim's total compliance, who cannot help but be compliant. Recognizing that this is happening is therefore the first necessary breach in the fences our mental enclosures have erected.

Enclosure usurps the categories of existence and disparages the concept of aliveness as well as the dimensions of experience linked to it. The practices of conceptual enclosure preemptively deny the existence of an unavailable other, making it impossible to conceptualize and honor real, subjective experience. This other is not only nature or a person from a foreign culture; it is the experience of a dimension of reality that can only be lived and not captured by rational conceptualization. This other is the domain of physically experienced reality that precedes all conceptualization and colonization: It is the bliss we experience when watching the sun rise or seeing a beloved partner or a puppy, or the dimension of meaning in a piece of work that benefits everyone and not just ourselves. It is the domain of what Manfred Max-Neef catalogs as "human needs"—the existential dimensions of healthy relationships to one's self and others.[11]

Enclosure occurs through a type of thinking that ignores creative processes and the meanings of emotions, both of which originate in the body. Enclosure instead subordinates these feelings to rationality, stewardship, empiricism, discursivity, and control. Such thinking culminates in the idea that the more-than-human-world and the body themselves do not exist, but are solely artifacts of culture. In modern society, it is considered naïve to believe that living otherness can be truly experienced as a domain of creative unfolding, or that there is a perceptible kinship of being alive that is shared by all living things and which can be experienced. Our cognitive frameworks and our use of language deny this reality, which amounts to a mental and spiritual enclosure. But the colonization of our innermost essence inescapably results in what biophilosopher David Kidner describes as being an "empty self."[12]

This de facto empty self is indeed diagnosed by many as a psychopathological "civilizational narcissism" that marks our times. In humanity's resurgent obsession with treating the Earth as a raw, inert resource (e.g., geoengineering to forestall climate change, synthetic biology to "improve upon" nature, etc.), the Enlightenment is making one last push for sovereignty over the cosmos. Here the Anthropocene is completely identical with anthropocentrism. The old notions of human superiority, control, and technical mastery are concealed by the equation of humans with nature, putting them on an equal footing.

Even a sophisticated theorist such as Bruno Latour falls for this category error when he reassures his readers: "The sin is not to wish to have dominion over nature but to believe that this dominion means emancipation and not attachment."[13] Since people are in fact connected through relationships (with the Earth, with each other), the fallacy lies in their attempting to dominate what embraces them in ways they do not understand; they are blind to reality and prone to act destructively.

Italian philosopher Ugo Mattei believes that even the act of dividing the world into subject and object results in the commodification of both.[14] The commodification of the spirit inevitably finds its warped expression at the real and political level. Nature is banished to the periphery of the human world even though it still nourishes and sustains us, produces everything we eat, and remains the wellspring of creative energy. Every separation into subject and object divides the world into two realms: resources and profiteers. This boundary is not necessarily between things and people (or between matter and creatures), but between what (or who) is consumed and those who benefit from that consumption.

Thus, we are suffering not only because of the commodification of the natural and social world. We are suffering because our conceptualization of the world itself allows commodification to stand as the sole way of relating to it. It is no longer possible to speak about the world via categories of subjective aliveness. We are suffering because of the enclosure of the spiritual through myriad cultural fictions of separation and domination that falsely parse the world into an outside (resources) and inside (actors). Concepts such as strict cause-and-effect relationships, causal mechanisms, the separation of body and soul—all of them fundamental premises to enlightenment thinking—result in our taking reality hostage. We colonize it by believing in the concept of a treatable, repairable, controllable world. Any experience that contradicts this enclosure of reality must be discounted or denied.

Yet most of us are unaware of the profoundly misleading taxonomic screens of our language and worldview. We can barely imagine the extent to which our view of reality is distorted by spiritual enclosure. We fail to realize that the self-organizing nature of our everyday lives has disappeared. Yet this dispossession is far more radical than the one experienced by commoners locked out of their forests a few hundred years ago. We fail to appreciate how conceiving of our own selves as biomachines has impoverished us as humans, and how treating disturbing emotions chiefly as "chemical imbalances" (to be corrected through pharmaceuticals) denies an elemental dimension of our humanity.

Cutting living subjects off from participating in the commons of reality and its mixture of practices and emotions, objects and aspects of meaning, is destructive in another serious respect: it blinds us to the nature of enclosure itself. The overarching ideology of enclosure is an ideology of control and dominance, and a denial of enduring relationships. This systemic worldview is not only unjust and dangerous; it brazenly defies reality.

THE FERTILITY OF WASTEFULNESS

What are the most prominent biological flaws of our bioeconomic view? How does it misrepresent actual biology? Which myths about life does it create that cannot be validated by reality? What can we say about the validity of the common assumptions of the bioeconomic paradigm? Most if not all of them ignore the fact that we are living subjects in a living world continuously brought forth by subjective, creative agents. The orthodox assumptions of bioeconomics already violate the state-of-the-art research in the physical sciences that shows that no relationships between subjects and objects are possible if you clearly separate the observer and the observed. What observations in ecology—the natural household—could encourage a shift to an economic *enlivenment*?

The prevailing biological view of the organic world—and the picture of human beings within it—is changing. New research is shifting the paradigm from the Darwinian idea of a battlefield between antagonistic survival-machines to that of a complex interplay among various agents with conflicting and symbiotic goals and meanings. In the new biological paradigm, the organism is starting to be seen as a subject that *interprets* external stimuli and genetic influences rather than being causally governed by them. An organism negotiates the terms of its existence with others under conditions of limited competition and "weak causality." This shift in the axioms of "biological liberalism" is opening up a new picture of the organic world as one in which freedom evolves and organisms, including humans, play an active, constructive role in imagining and building new futures. The natural world as it actually works *refutes* many axioms of the bio-economic worldview.

Efficiency

The biosphere is not efficient. Warm-blooded animals consume over 97 percent of their energy just to maintain their metabolism. Photosynthesis achieves a ridiculously low efficiency rate of 3–6 percent, far inferior to technical photoenergetic solutions. Fish, amphibians, and insects have to produce millions of fertilized eggs just to allow a very few offspring to survive. Parsimony is simply not to be found in nature. Instead of being sparing and efficient, nature is highly wasteful. It compensates for possible loss through massive squandering. Biological organization is enabled through "order for free" (Stuart Kauffman),[15] through structures that are not efficient but which simply arise on their own accord through certain constellations that are often characterized by high degrees of disorder. The biosphere itself is based on a "donation," the foundation of all biological work—solar energy—which comes to us as a gift from heaven.

Growth
The biosphere does not grow. The total quantity of biomass does not increase. The throughput of matter does not expand; nature runs a steady-state economy—that is, an economy in which all relevant factors remain constant in relation to each other. Nor does the number of species necessarily increase; it rises in some epochs and falls in others. The only dimension that really grows is the diversity of experiences: ways of feeling, modes of expression, variations of appearance, novelties in patterns and forms. Therefore, nature gains neither mass nor weight, but rather depth. This is not a dimension that can be evaluated and quantified, however. It is a poetic expression of a sediment of desire that is either frustrated or fulfilled.

Competition
It has never been possible to prove empirically that a new species has arisen over competition for a resource alone.

Rather, species are born by chance: they develop through unexpected mutations and the isolation of a group from the rest of the population through new symbioses and cooperation (the process by which our body cells arose from bacterial predecessors cooperating in intracellular symbiosis, for example). Competition alone—for example, for a limited nutrient or ecological niche—causes biological monotony: the dominance of relatively few species over an ecosystem.[16]

Scarcity

Resources in nature are not scarce. Where they become so, scarcity does not lead to a creative diversification, but to an impoverishment of diversity and freedom. The basic energy resource of nature—sunlight—exists in abundance. A second crucial resource—the number of ecological relationships and new niches—has no upper limit. Relationships increase not through parsimony, but through sharing. A high number of species and a variety of relations among them lead not to sharper competition and dominance of a "fitter" species, but rather to richer permutations of relationships among species and thus to an increase in freedom, which is at the same time also an increase in mutual dependencies. The more that resources are "wasted" (consumed by other species), the bigger the common wealth becomes. Life has the tendency to transform all available resources into a meshwork of bodies. In old ecosystems in which solar energy is constant, as in tropical rainforests, high oceans of the lower latitudes and tropical coastal ecosystems, this tendency manifests itself as an increase in niches and thus as a higher overall diversity. The result is an upsurge of symbioses and reduced competition. Scarcity of resources, as the cyclical lack of specific nutrients, leads to less diversity and the dominance of few species, as can be observed in temperate ocean mudflats.

Scarcity does not exist in indigenous thinking. In traditional societies, it might exist as phenomenon, but not as concept. True shortages can occur, particularly in winter or during dry seasons, but they do not lead to an increase in the "price" of resources, as these are neither bartered nor traded but shared. Scarcity in indigenous societies thus leads to a higher degree of sharing. Scarcity leads not to limiting resources but to recycling them through intricate ways of redistribution. Food-sharing rituals, which are found not only in human Stone-Age cultures but also among canids, can be seen as examples of this, as can the fact that the extraordinarily high degree of ecological niches in tropical environments is a way to reuse and redistribute limited nutrients such as phosphorus and nitrogen. Bartering caused by ostensible scarcity therefore acts against the necessary processes of the biosphere. The economic value achieved through scarcity is directly opposed to any real or ecological value. Ecological scarcity can only be brought about through property. Therefore, property violates ecological laws.

Property

There is no notion of property in the biosphere. Individuals do not even possess their own bodies. Bodies' matter changes continuously as it is replaced by oxygen, carbon, and other inputs of energy and matter. But it is not only the physical dimension of the self that is made possible through its material communion with other elements and thus through a form of unity of existential dependency and powerlessness. The absence of property among life-giving forces holds for the symbolic sphere as well. Language is brought forth by the community of speakers who use it and, in using it, create self-awareness and identity. Habits in a species are acquired by sharing them among individuals. In sleep, in birth, in love, and in all emotions, we do not entirely own ourselves, but are overtaken. And only in these passions, in states of bliss or pain, do we truly become ourselves.

In any of these dimensions, the wildness of the natural world is necessary if the individual is to develop its innermost identity. The self-organizing creative power of reality allows individuality to unfold from underlying contradictions in order to build its own distinctiveness. This world *becomes*; it is not made by any particular individual, nor can it be exclusively possessed. Individuality in its physical, social, and symbolic sense can emerge only through a biologically shared and culturally communicated commons. Identity is a commons. This narrative's respective narrators—you, I, and all beings—are forever a part of what is happening, and at the same time always create their own plot.

3 BIOPOETICS: DESIRING TO BE

I did not develop the preceding ideas out of thin air.[1] A new framework for biological thinking that favors the reality of biological agents is currently taking over empirical research. In the emerging new biological paradigm, aliveness is a notion and an experience that governs the perceptions of biological agents. Subjectivity is a biological driving force. "Commoning" is a metabolic reality. The body itself—our own individual bodies, for that matter—is possible only through participation in reality as a commons.

Two decades ago, writing in the journal *Science*, the molecular biologist Richard Strohmann foresaw a paradigm shift in biology that he termed the "organic turn in biology."[2] By 2018, many of his assumptions have been empirically confirmed. The theoretical foundations of the classical molecular-evolutionary model in biology have now been called into question and are being interpreted in a new light. Biology is undergoing a profound reassessment of its core premises, much as physics was transformed when relativity and quantum theory were discovered about a century ago.

There is one significant difference, however: the changes in theoretical biology are not yet culturally recognized. On the contrary, the dogma of bioeconomics, as described in the last chapter, has never been more influential than it is today. Mainstream biology, as it is taught in school and university classes, and as it is vulgarized in the mass media, continues to occupy the popular imagination.

But at the frontiers of original thinking in the biological sciences, deep, conceptual change is taking place. The Newtonian doctrine of a genetic blueprint commanding a machine-like organic system while constantly striving for new efficiencies driven by the laws of natural selection is no longer confirmed in many areas of research. Rather, biologists are beginning to observe a living world consisting of interrelated subjects who are sentient and expressive of this sentience, which manifests itself in (inner) experiences and (external) behaviors.

The behavior of organisms, hitherto understood as basically determined by the execution of genetic orders within the framework of a specific environment, has gained an unheard of degree of freedom in actual biological research. It can even change DNA. Epigenetic regulation plays a much more important role than previously thought, which means that individual organisms can influence the fate of their own genes.[3] It is now well established that parental experiences can be passed on genetically[4] and that even cultural practices in child rearing may directly influence children's genomes.[5] The emerging, more holistic paradigm of biological regulation now holds that the identity of biological subjects is often not that of one species alone: the majority of organisms must be viewed as "metabiomes" consisting of thousands of symbiotic, mostly bacterial species, according to recent research.[6]

EMPIRICAL SUBJECTIVITY

An organism is not a single autonomous subject but must be regarded as a kind of ecosystem—as a "super-organism" built from innumerable cellular "selves." A given organism is not simply the result of a linear cascade of causes and subsequent effects. Current views in empirical biological research, particularly in developmental genetics, proteomics, and systems biology, are beginning to appreciate self-production and autopoiesis as central features of living beings. (*Autopoeiesis*, literally "self-creation," is a term introduced by Chilean biologists Humberto Maturana and Francisco Varela to describe the capacity of an organism to continuously generate and specify its own organization autonomously.[7]) Researchers are increasingly discussing genetic coding and developmental and regulatory processes in terms of an organism's capacity to interpret and experience biological meaning and subjectivity.[8]

These findings not only challenge the standard empirical approach to organisms; they transform our underlying assumptions about what life is. Is an organism a machine, assembled from parts that have to be viewed as still smaller machines or subassemblies? Or is life a phenomenon in which subjectivity, interpretation, and existential need are key forces that cannot be excluded from the picture without distorting our understanding of how an organism functions and without obstructing the path to further explanations?

In the emerging new picture, organisms are no longer viewed as genetic machines, but basically as materially embodied processes that determine themselves.[9] They are matter, organization, but also meaning, existential experience, and poetic expression. Each single cell is a "process of creation of an identity."[10] Even the simplest organism must be understood as a material system displaying the desire to keep itself intact, to grow, to unfold, and to produce a fuller scope of life for itself. A cell is a process that produces the components necessary for these developments—while the materials of carbon, nitrogen, oxygen, phosphorus, and silicon flow through it.

The cell is not a material unity, but a meaningful self that produces its own identity through the continued desire to be whole through connection to other matter. A cell is not a tiny machine acting on genetic orders. Its basic activity instead consists in the ever-ongoing production of its own components. The insistent drive toward the maintenance of its own self, which we can witness in other life forms, and which we can recognize also drives ourselves through our experience of the joy of living, if successfully realized, is to keep going as this specific identity. This has one central consequence that makes the enlivened picture of biology so different from its predecessors: an embodied self that intends to keep itself intact automatically develops interests, a standpoint, and hence, subjectivity. It is a subject with a body. If natural history is the unfolding of selves, it no longer makes sense to speak of organisms as machines without individual, felt, and expressed interests, as is customary in bioeconomics. Subjectivity is no illusion in the service of maximizing success, but the way through which biological existence is possible in the first place. We can see it in bodies and we can experience it in ourselves. Only if it includes this experience, not only as theoretical elaboration but as a practice of doing, can the scope of science encompass reality as a whole. In order to objectively grasp embodied existence, it is necessary to be a subject.

THE NATURAL HISTORY OF FREEDOM

Let me sum up the traits of this new framework for conceptualizing the principles that guide a living being.

A living being acts according to its own autonomy, and therefore is not completely determined by external factors. It creates its identity by transforming matter into the stuff of self.

It produces itself and thereby manifests the desire to grow, avoid conflict, and actively search for positive inputs such as food, shelter, and the presence of companions.

It is constantly evaluating influences from the external (and also its own internal) world.

It follows goals.

It acts out of concern and from the experience of meaning.

It is an agent or a subject with an intentional point of view. We can call this way of meaning-guided world-making *feeling*.

It shows or expresses the conditions under which its life process takes place. A living being transparently exhibits its conditions.

It unfolds as the poetic imagination of the meaning of its existence.

It partakes in an experience encompassing all beings, which we could call *conditio vitae*—the condition of life and the fact that we are all alive through one another.

The *conditio vitae* is the fundamental common ground for all organisms. It encompasses the principles of living creativity in nonverbal and nonalgorithmic ways. The *conditio vitae* is the basic shared poetic condition, because it shows the basic laws of agency and embodiment that are also manifestly in ourselves as human beings. Every organism is an expression of the conditions of existence.

Only from this new perspective on life can we find paramount principles and their according attitudes that pave the way for reciprocal and cooperative processes and hence enable aliveness. Our picture of reality, which finds its expression in a living biosphere, follows these primordial principles of organic transformations:

Natural history should be viewed not as the functioning of some kind of organic machine, but rather as the unfolding of a natural history of freedom, experience, and agency.

Reality is alive. It is full of subjective experience and feeling.

Subjective experience and feeling are prerequisites of rationality.

The biosphere consists of the material, metabolic, and meaningful interrelations of selves.

The individual can exist only if the whole exists and the whole can exist only if individuals are allowed to exist.

Embodied selves come into being only through others. The biosphere critically depends on cooperation and "interbeing"—the idea that a self is not possible in isolation and through a frenetic struggle of all against all, but is from the very beginning dependent on the other—in the form of food, shelter, companions. Self is only self through other. In human development, this is very clear, as the infant must be seen and positively valued by its caretakers if it is to develop a healthy self.

The biosphere is paradoxically cooperative. Symbiotic relationships emerge out of antagonistic, incompatible processes: matter/form, genetic code/soma, individual ego/other. Incompatibility is necessary for life in the first place, and therefore any living existence can only be precarious and preliminary—an improvised creative solution for the moment.[11] Existence comes into being through transitory negotiations of several incompatible layers of life. In this sense, living systems are always a self-contradictory "meshwork of selfless selves."[12]

The experience of being fully alive, of being joyful, is a fundamental component of reality. The desire for experience and to become one's own full self is a general rule of "biological worldmaking," which consists of both the interior/experiential and the exterior/material construction of a self.

The living process is open. Although there are general rules for maintaining an embodied identity in interbeing, its form is entirely subject to situational solutions.

There is no neutral transhistorical information, no general "scientific" objectivity. There is only a common experiential level of understanding, interbeing, and communion of a shared *conditio vitae*. New structures and levels of enlivenment can be made possible through acts of reciprocal imagination.

Death is real. Death is inevitable and even necessary as the precondition for the individual's striving to stay intact and to grow. Death is an integral component of life. We should talk, rather, of *death/birth* when referring to the whole of life as organic reality.

EMBODIED OBJECTIVITY

From these observations, it seems possible to complete the highly limited mainstream ecological worldview that still prevails (nature viewed as an exterior pool of resources) with an interior or intentional aspect. To the scientific third-person perspective of "objective reality" we must add a first-person ecology. Therefore, the empirical objectivity that is so familiar to contemporary science must be enlarged by an "empirical subjectivity"—a shared condition of feeling and experience among all living beings. This empirical subjectivity conveys insights that can be generalized, although in a weak sense, not in the "measured and counted" way of empirical objectivity. Empirical subjectivity accordingly yields an embodied or "poetic" objectivity as a way of expressing itself (for a deeper discussion of poetic objectivity, see chapter 7).

Empirical subjectivity is what makes the perception of others possible. It includes the subjective impression conveyed by mirror neurons that makes one feel in one's own body the joy or pain another being feels. It works through the existential meanings all living beings share because they are mortal and have vulnerable bodies. Empirical subjectivity is objective in the sense that it relies on the values created by embodied aliveness, which are fundamentally shared by all embodied beings. The object of empirical subjectivity is the *conditio vitae*, the condition of life. The bodies of others are transparent to other bodies in a nonverbal way. They show what is happening to them on an existential level.[13] Empirical subjectivity is the primary vehicle for creating meaning and transmission in the biological world. For this reason, "metaphors are the logic of the organic world," as Gregory Bateson put it—the binding glue of organic processes.[14]

The objectivity that is shared through having the same kind of body—and being part of one unique metabolism of the biosphere—comes with a poetic aspect to it. This objectivity can be objective only insofar as it is poetic, which is to say, felt in an individual body that is nonetheless matter belonging to that world and part of a shared whole. True objectivity from this standpoint is tied to poetic perception. This means that insights that have been excluded by the "objective-only" position—because they are not real in a material, physical sense—may very well be valid in a poetic, "interior" sense.

Bateson describes this meaning generation process when he compares classical ("objective") logic with the ("abductive") form of logic that is embodied and subjective. The understanding gained through this latter form of logic is what rules the biological world, including the human sphere. The logical argument that Bateson offers is the classic:

1. Men are mortal.

2. Socrates is a man.

3. Socrates is mortal.

The poetic argument, however, allows for an experience not already contained in the premises. It is a speculative insight. This insight rests on shared empirical subjectivity and enables an immediate knowledge, which is impossible to convey otherwise. It contains what Bateson calls "the pattern that connects," which is poetic objectivity:

1. Men are mortal.

2. Grass is mortal.

3. Men are grass.[15]

This insight, of course, is not literally true. It is true, however, as an experiential, or poetic, insight. As a poetic insight, it must not be true. Still, it conveys knowledge about being a part of the living world. The truth of the poetic statement, therefore, rests on the fact that it is false. Its truth comes through its paradoxical nature. It refers to real experience, to the experience of a living body that knows how much it shares with other living bodies, which in a strange way are the same, but are also different.

Insights of this kind can change our behavior and in this sense are an influential element of our living reality. They can let us see truths beyond our current understanding because they act from where we are not, from where we are linked with the world. "And if the world has ceased to hear you, / say to the silent earth: I flow. / To the rushing water, speak: I am," writes the poet Rainer Maria Rilke in the very last of his *Sonnets to Orpheus*. The poet here speaks from the knowledge that men are at once grass and the water that nourishes the grassroots. This mode of understanding inhabits an intimate distance. It stems from the encounter with the fact of one's being the world split unto itself and reunited through longing: I am you, because I am your opposite, that for which you are yearning.

The poetical dimension is that dimension of our organic existence which we most deeply deny. It is the world of our feelings, of our social bonds, and of everything else that we experience as significant and meaningful. The denied poetic dimension is part and parcel of our everyday world of social communication, linked to our exchanges and interactions, to laughter and consternation, to the needs of our flesh. It is the world of the first-person perspective, which is always there, and is always felt and experienced. It is the world that we live in most intimately, and it is ultimately the world for which we conceive and make various policies. The economic exchange, which is a social give-and-take between living beings, also takes place in this world.

4 NATURAL ANTICAPITALISM: EXCHANGE AS RECIPROCITY

Enlivenment means getting back to living reality as an inspiration and understanding for all areas of science. Its essence is to reincorporate the vibrant, poetic, felt, speculative, and imaginative reality. To find one's bearings in this kind of reality requires contagion—and is therefore the opposite of essentialism.

Enlivenment enables individual and collective identity, because it admits for the biophysical necessity as well as for the poetic freedom that is inscribed into it. This framing of living existence as an "enlivened integration" of necessity and freedom does not mean "copying" the supposedly deterministic laws of nature and applying them to questions of ethics or culture. Instead, it reasserts a seemingly obvious fact—that manmade structures and practices of human societies are the creations of living beings in a living world. To maintain our connection to this living world, we need to respect its basic principles of fertility and mutual exchange, which are already structuring the unconscious workings of our bodies, namely our metabolism and our emotions. Enlivenment means unfolding as a living part in a vibrant household of energy flows and meanings. It means recreating any relationship of reciprocity in an honest and fertile way. It means striving for freedom by giving in to necessity.

This shift of perspective has implications for economic science. The double metaphor of eco-nomy/logy, if applied in a proper, nonreductionist way, offers a perspective for seeing all living household processes, ecological or human, from the same angle. Unlike previous attempts to naturalize economics with biological justifications—the essence of social Darwinism and neoliberalism—enlivenment looks to biological systems to understand the default patterns of self-organized flows of matter and information in their existential dimension, and includes the interior perspective through which living systems unfold.

Here we come to realize that exchange processes in living, ecological spheres are neither efficiency oriented nor controlled by external forces that render individuals impotent and without agency. Nor are the spheres of the living bereft of intentionality, sense, or self; they are instead a paradoxical and always embodied combination of different levels of selves realizing themselves through material and meaning-based exchanges.

If economic theory is unburdened of its Darwinian-optimization content, and if the notion of the market is exchanged for the idea of the household of and with the biosphere, we can see more clearly how economic processes that enhance life could be made fertile for ourselves. We can even see that a certain form of householding, which is undergoing a huge renaissance at the moment, is clearly favored by nature: the economy of the commons.[1]

From the standpoint of enlivenment, nature is a commons economy consisting of subjects who are continuously mediating relationships between one another, relationships that have a material side, but also always embody meaning, lived sense, and the notion of belonging to a place. A commons economy, to repeat my definition from the beginning of the introduction, is a household in which there are no users in disposition of resources, but embodied agents creating the fertility of the world through the way they re-enact the primal creative relationships that bring forth life.

STONE AGE ECONOMICS

It is interesting to note that "primitive" and prehistoric "economies"—ways of providing food, shelter, and of relating to the environment—are for the most part full-blown commons economies.[2] This type of householding can be regarded as the default setting for the ways humans distribute the material goods necessary for living. "Active partaking in the ecological commons" is therefore the most fitting description of the original human economic activities. But to speak of economic activities here is misleading. Early humans as well as contemporary indigenous peoples do not think in terms of economy, but in terms of fertility: their activities are meant to keep the cosmos alive, and through this provide themselves with a part of the cosmos's life-giving force. Original peoples do not have an economic mindset. They do not strive for growth, or for optimization of any kind. They desire to fulfill the rules that lead to fertility, and these are the rules that are valid for the unfolding of ecosystems.

This observation changes the mainstream narrative of how markets arose in history. Historians tend to ascribe to humans a universal tendency to trade and negotiate as a response to an ostensible universal scarcity. But humans do not barter by default, contrary to the myths of the origin of the market economy that have been told to students all over the world for decades. In most early societies, humans experience themselves as participating in a generous cosmos that distributes its gifts to them and needs to be given back in reciprocity in order to keep it productive. Human householding has developed as a metabolism with a bountiful world that yearns to come more alive. That would be the most accurate description of the "state of nature." The state of nature is centered on the art of being a fruitful part of an ecosystem. It is not about humans trading material goods.

In the state of nature, the most important prerequisite for economy does not even exist: the neat separation of human affairs from the rest of the world, imagined as a set of objects. Instead, humans are actors in a living cosmos made up of relationships that blossom if they are honored in the right way. Many archaic cultures do not even differentiate between "nature" and "culture," or "animate" and "inanimate"; the two are organically integrated within a single worldview.[3] Nor do they differentiate their ways of relating to ecosystems from the way they treat human relationships. Their modes of thinking and perceiving integrate a multitude of players that are continuously entangled in interactions. In the indigenous cosmos, everything is alive and able to engage in reciprocal relationships.

The principles of exchange in primitive societies, commons economies, and natural ecosystems are strikingly similar. In all three, transformational processes have to be brought into dynamic alignment with external factors. This helps explain why the cultures of commons-based systems often mirror the cosmic exchange systems of natural eco-systems. Social bonds evolved to become part and parcel of the ecosystem.

In Western thought, however, nature has for several centuries been regarded as the other—the unfathomably evil and wild forces of the world that we can only protect ourselves against by imposing a disciplined "crust" of in-stitutional civilization. Hence the assumption that without institutions we would immediately fall back into barba-rism, which the prominent historian Timothy Garton Ash made in an analysis on the (false) reports of violence in the wake of the hurricane Katrina disaster in New Or-leans.[4] The idea that the state is the only reliable barrier against barbarism is forcefully rebutted by Rebecca Solnit in her study of people's transcendently kind and coura-geous behaviors as a response to natural catastrophes and human accidents.[5]

For millennia, human societies understood the bio-sphere as a commons-based economy and treated their internal cultures, material resources, and immaterial exchange relations as a part of a huge, all-encompassing commons. Modern industrial cultures typically condescend to such "primitive" economies by dismissing their "supersti-tions" and extolling the virtues of objective science. But who is being naïve and parochial? The behavior of such societies reflects deep insights into the meaning of ecological and existential reality. It is the "moderns" who have profoundly lost touch with insights into the principles underlying life.

We must admit that a huge part of Enlightenment political philosophy—ideas about the state of nature and the social contract—laid the ground for colonial rule. These ideas sought to legitimate the delegation of powers, starting from a simply wrong assumption about the way humans organize their relationships with one another and with the cosmos. Here again we find the *petitio principii* that is the herald of dualism: the Enlightenment philosophers started from their own historical experience in order to imagine a "neutral" idea of man beyond all social relationships. They projected back the evil they experienced in their own highly hierarchic societies onto the picture they painted of the state of nature of early humans.

The central premise was the absence of relations and the separation of the essence of humankind from the objects of nature, which then needed domination in order to be fruitfully exploited. What in universities today is still taught as the foundation of modern political—and democratic—theories, is in its core a wrong idea about the cosmos. This idea serves to subjugate parts of the world in order to legitimize the existence of a small class of rulers. The domination of nature as other and the dominance of the idea that humans are *ipso facto* separated from the rest of the universe come to the same thing. Therefore, Enlightenment political philosophy carried the germ of totalitarianism in its core. Much of it until today, including even John Rawls's theory of justice,[6] has dealt with the unruly state of brutal nature that must be kept in check through a social contract. Seen from that standpoint, Enlightenment philosophy is in large part a theory of colonialism.

The human propensity for interacting with material things on a social basis—and not just through impersonal, cash-mediated market relations—is the hallmark of a commons. But it is also the promise of an attitude toward the world with which we are connected materially through our own metabolism on the one hand, and attached through a host of meanings on the other.

The economy of the commons therefore holds promise for building a more sustainable future. It represents the building blocks of an embodied economy in which humans are tightly integrated with the more-than-human-world. The ecological and psychological realism inherent in this worldview holds many lessons for us today. Any economy must give us the feeling of connection and participation. For human actors *are* materially a part of the world they are dealing with, and their individual experiences of meaning derive from the ways in which their material interactions are organized. Only an economy that includes nonhuman beings and the land will not play material exchange processes and meaningful human relationships against each other.

THE CIRCLE OF THE GIFT

From an enlivenment standpoint, nature itself is a commons. It consists of subjects that are constantly negotiating their relationships. These relationships have a material basis, but they also communicate meaning and carry a sense of belonging to a particular place.

Nature, understood as a creative process of interacting embodied subjects, can serve as a model for an economic concept of the commons. Basic structures and principles of "natural commoning"—self-organizing, dynamic, creative— have been the basis for biospherical evolution. I argue that the principles of self-organization in nature provide a template for any commons economy. These principles follow the basic outlines of all transformational relationships in the biosphere. They do not augur stale harmony, however, but only become operative through paradox, which does not promise salvation, but requires—and enables—continuous gestures of imagination.

Bioeconomy	Life
Identities	Relationships
Empiricism	Empirical subjectivity
Abstraction	Poetic objectivity
Information	Feeling
Outside or inside	Outside as inside
Separation	Imagination
Constraints	Needs
Contest	Mutual gifts
Description	Participation
Barter	Transformation
Control	Commons
Dualism	Biopoetics

COMMONS AS A PRACTICE OF REALITY IN THE FIRST PERSON

The guidelines of this reciprocal productivity are:

General principles, local rules

Every patch of living earth functions by the same ecological principles—but each one is still a unique individual realization of these principles. There are different rules for flourishing in a temperate forest, for example, than in an arid desert. Each ecosystem is the integral of many rules, interactions, and streams of matter, which share common principles but are locally unique. General rules must be imagined in a distinctive way every time.

Interbeing

The primeval principle of the living world is, as naturalist John Muir put it: "Everything is hitched to everything else."[7] In the ecological commons, a multitude of different individuals and diverse species stand in various relationships to one another—competition and cooperation, partnership and predatory hostility, productivity and destruction. All those relations, however, follow one higher law: only behavior that allows for the productivity of the whole ecosystem over the long term and does not interrupt its capacities of self-production can survive and expand. The individual is able to realize itself only if the whole can realize itself. Ecological freedom obeys this basic necessity. The deeper the connections in the system, the more creative niches it will offer its individual members. New species can alter the equilibrium of an existing system, opening up novel opportunities for growth and innovation. On the other hand, if the "fitness landscape" changes for some reason, individuals of a certain species may have access to fewer and fewer resources and eventually go extinct. Keystone species—for example, large herbivores in temperate grasslands—provide an anchor for the equilibrium of a whole landscape. Large herbivores need savannas to thrive—which, in turn, must be grazed to remain intact.

You are the commons

Living beings do not "use" the commons provided by nature. Instead, they are physically and relationally a part of it. Participants in a commons digest the commons and provide nourishment for it at the same time. The individual's existence and the commons as a system are mutually interdependent. They cannot be set apart—just as you cannot differentiate body and embodied meaning, nor gesture and the signification expressed through it. The quality, health, and beauty of a commons system are based on a precarious balance that has to be negotiated from one moment to the next. Individual organisms cannot have too much autonomy lest they destabilize the commons by becoming free riders, overexploiting the system, like pests such as the crown-of-thorns starfish disease in tropical coral reefs do. From a commons point of view, events that we currently call "ecological catastrophes" and probably even diseases are manifestations of the free-rider phenomenon, which creates an imbalance in powers among an ecological commons. One participant or a particular group of them no longer partakes in reciprocity—as human civilization on the whole has ceased to do today. Conversely, insufficient wiggle room in the law of reciprocity can be equally ruinous. The global system must not impose overly strict or hostile controls lest it interfere with the productive processes of the system (e.g., heavy use of fertilizers or pesticides that disrupt natural processes). Animals transported to far-off and isolated regions such as the Galapagos Islands can alter whole ecosystems and start a new territorial narrative of biological history. Here the existing climatic and biogeographical features and the evolutionary potential of newcomers mutually transform one another. The simple lesson is: we cannot separate the individual from the whole. They are both parts of one bigger picture and "reciprocally specify" (as Varela puts it)[8] one another. But neither side is ever dissolved in the other.

Resources are meaning

Throughout natural history, ecosystems have developed multiple patterns of dynamic balance that lead to extraordinary refinement and high levels of aesthetic beauty. The forms and beings of nature amount to ingenious improvisations for maintaining delicate balances in a complex system. The beauty of living things stems from the fact that they are embodied solutions of individual-existence-in-connection. They are gradients expressive of the perennial paradox between total autonomy and complete fusion that needs to be held in suspense by every living being. In the material presence of an organism, such a solution presents itself as a "gesture of aliveness." It is immediately plausible for us, fellow living beings, but it never can be fully explained. It needs to be shared by our own presence, by our own partaking. As such, the experience of beauty is a necessary ingredient of a commoning process. It explains why most humans experience feelings of belonging and connection with other living beings. In them, the paradox of existence as individual-in-connection has been resolved in a poetic way, and at the same time presented as a new mystery—not as an answer, but as a question that compels one to seek the right response.

Reciprocity

Systems within a dynamic equilibrium are healthy, that is, novelty-producing and self-stabilizing at the same time. If disruptions or damage cause more stress than the individual, community, or species is able to endure, the resilience of the whole weakens. The "balance level" is not a fixed threshold, but more of a zone for absorbing what Varela and Maturana call "disruptive perturbation."[9] The degree of a system's tolerance for stress is difficult to diagnose in an objective manner and even more difficult to predict. We need to view stress not only as an objective blockade, but as a crisis of imagination: as something that impedes the ability to undergo transformation. Stress that exceeds the structural resilience of the system results in the system being unable to produce a "surplus of meaning"[10]—it cannot provide its gifts to other parts of the ecosystem, and it can no longer transform itself. Health, therefore, is not harmony, but the ability to develop creative relationships. This is often forgotten when we define a disease or a disturbance. We tend to confuse the outward appearance of health with the inner dimension of productive creativity, which might seem rather chaotic from the outside. Aliveness, however, is not chaotic. Health does not mean static equilibrium or "homeostasis"; it is a dynamic negotiation among the system's elements over exactly how far the system can stretch to accommodate stress. Stress can actually stimulate as long as it remains within ecotone-levels (an ecotone is the patchy fringe between two or more specific areas area of a system). Beyond that, disruptions can become devastating for the whole and eventually destroy it. On the larger system level, this destruction will lead to a new equilibrium, but not with the same players as before.

No copyright

Nothing in nature can be exclusively owned or controlled; nothing in nature is a monopoly. Everything is open source. The quintessence of the organic realm is not the selfish gene but the openly available source code of genetic information that can be used by all. The genes being patented today by biocorporations are nonrival and nonexclusive in a biological sense. They cannot be owned. This is proven by the "superweeds" that have emerged from the large-scale culture of genetically modified crops. They demonstrate that patented genes are under no ownership. Biological "information" (which is actually the variation among individualized ways of partaking in the give-and-take of ecosystems) belongs—like sunlight, like water, like the mineral skin of the earth—to all. It is abundant, not scarce. DNA has been able to branch into so many species only because all sorts of organisms can use its code, tinker with it, and derive combinations that are meaningful and useful. This is also the way *Homo sapiens* came about: Nature was playing around with open source code. Some 20 percent of our genome alone consists of former viral genes that have been creatively recycled.

Gift exchange

As there is no property in nature, there is no waste. All waste products are literally food for some other member of the ecological community. Every individual offers itself at death as a gift to be feasted upon by others, in the same way it received the gifts of the bodies of others, and of sunlight, to sustain its existence. We can understand death as being the freedom to give oneself to the community one day. There remains a largely unexplored connection between giving and taking in ecosystems in which loss is the precondition for generativity.

ECOLOGICAL SELF-REALIZATION

A thorough analysis of the economy of ecosystems can yield powerful guidelines for new types of enlivened economy—an economy based on the commons. We should look to natural processes—as expressions of the natural history of freedom—to guide our thinking as to how to transform the embodied, material aspect of our existence into a culture of being alive.

The theory of the commons I am outlining here provides a theory of the principles of reciprocity. This theory can integrate the distinction between "material" and "social" and between "functional" and "emotional." Every practice of the commons is an existential description of reality. It relinquishes the common dualisms of the Enlightenment (culture–nature, alive–inanimate, etc.) because it takes up more than just a theoretical perspective. In this sense, it is "posthuman": humankind is not understood as a sovereign ruler, but as one occupying a shifting position in a network of relationships in which all actions feed back to the agent, and in which they feed back out to innumerable other positions and nodes that are also active—be they other human subjects, bats, fungi, bacteria, emotional states, contagions, or metaphors.

We should look at natural processes as the expression of the natural history of freedom and accordingly align our own actions with them. We should ponder how the embodied, material aspects of our existence can be answered by a culture that broadens the aliveness of the world. The term *commons* can help link the organic and sociocultural worlds in ways that deepen mutual understanding and bring them into greater coherence, even synergy. If we understand nature as an authentic, primal commons, we will develop a new self-understanding from a biological, social, and political perspective.

The term *commons* provides a conceptual binding that can help us conjoin the natural world (the self-producing world of beings and species) and the social-cultural domain (the things and processes brought forth by human beings through symbolic systems, discourses, and practices) and make them more compatible (if not synergistic). To understand nature as an authentic, aboriginal commons opens the way to a novel understanding of ourselves—in both a biological and social sense.

If nature actually is a commons, it follows that the only possible way to achieve a stable, long-term productive relationship with it is by building an economy of the commons. This can be the key to help dissolve the traditional duality of humans and nature, and orient us toward respectful, sustainable models of engaging with the more-than-human aspects of nature.

The self-realization of what Terrence Deacon describes as the "symbolic species,"[11] *Homo sapiens*, can be best achieved in a commons, simply because such a culture—and thus any socioeconomic system—is the species-specific realization of our own version of natural existence, of natural being as being self-in-connection. It is our individual cultural interpretation of the principles of the biosphere, not the dogged obedience to their demands. A culture of the commons is the productive, liberal interpretation of the principles that build the biosphere.

Although the deliberations that have led us to this point stem from a thorough analysis of biology, their results are not biologistic (in the sense of applying only to biological phenomena). Quite the opposite: analysis shows that the organic realm is the paradigm for the evolution of freedom. Natural principles may impose certain necessary parameters to life, but those principles are nondeterministic and allow for significant zones of creativity and freedom.

FREEDOM THROUGH NECESSITY

At this point it is necessary to look at a fundamental paradox in respect of the meaning of freedom. Freedom as it is understood by enlivenment differs from the view of freedom that neoliberalism propagates for the "free market." The latter is a freedom *from* necessities, which is to be achieved by risk control, the total quenching of material needs, and unhindered self-realization. Enlivened freedom is a freedom *through* necessities. This freedom becomes possible only by answering to inevitable constraints in a way that allows for their transformation through a fertile practice. To engage in restrictions equips an individual with autonomy. Or rather, imagining how to cope with restraints in a unique way creates the individual. Although an individual is an independent actor, the individual is totally dependent on the surrounding world of others: she relies on them in order to enjoy food, protection, and community. Freedom is achievable only as a negotiation of necessities.

The French psychologists Miguel Benasayag and Gérard Schmit observe this interrelation in their analysis of the present time as an "epoch of sad passions" (a term first used by Spinoza to describe self-destructive psychological states).[12] The authors diagnose a basic misunderstanding in our culture about the character of freedom. They track the key to this back to Aristotle. For Aristotle, a person who does not have any connections, who does not have a place, who can be used everywhere and at all times, is not free but a slave. A free person, on the other hand, has many ties and accordingly many commitments to others and with respect to the polis he or she lives in.

A living being is only free through bonds—the ties of metabolism to matter, the affiliation of the individual with the species, the attachment to a partner and to offspring, the bond between predator and prey, which tries to escape being eaten and therefore is on a continuous search for free spaces, materially and symbolically. Biological freedom therefore always presupposes negotiating. It is freedom-in-and-through-relation. It has not much to do with the idea of total freedom of the individual in the free-market approach. The *oikos* of nature, however, is the natural system whose constraints limit the individual's freedom, but on the other hand form the only source from which autonomy can flow.

This argument is a paradigmatic illustration of how an enlivenment approach can augment the Enlightenment position. The enlivened idea of freedom does not do away with the classical-humanistic account of autonomy (as strictly biologistic accounts do), but rather limits its absoluteness to an embodied relativity, or better yet, relatedness. There is no such thing as individual freedom detached from the living world, and any attempt to claim as much inevitably violates the necessities of embodied life, organic beings' living needs.

From an enlivenment viewpoint, freedom is a natural process. It is the active counterpart of the necessities essential for the functioning of bodies in ecosystems. Freedom is a process of imagination that sculpts the material and emotional dimensions of exchange in the commons of ecological reality, which includes the physiological, the social, the emotional, and the poetic. The commons is always householding and therefore is an economy, but it is always also emotional metabolism: metamorphosis.

The idea of the commons is therefore grounded in an intricate understanding of freedom and its relationship to the whole: the individual enjoys many options of self-realization but the only viable ones depend upon the flourishing of the life/social systems to which she belongs. The self can grow only through an unfolding of the other, and vice versa.

Therefore the secret of every loving bond is enclosed in the commons. Every productive relationship has the shape of a commons. To organize a community among humans and/or nonhuman agents according to the principles of the commons means to increase individual freedom by enlarging the community's freedom. Both expand together and mutually through one another, because expansion is possible only as a mutual transformation of both.

Contrary to what our dualistic culture supposes, reality is not divided into material substances of atoms and molecules on the one hand (governed by deterministic principles of biophysics) and nonmaterial culture/society (which are nondeterministic and mental/semiotic in character). The truth about living organisms is that they depend on a precarious balance between autonomy and relatedness to the whole on *all* levels of their functioning. Biological evolution is a creative process that produces rules for an increase of the whole through the self-realization of each of its members.

These rules are different for each time and each place, but we find them everywhere life exists. One could say, indeed, that they are the basic structures of any aliveness. They are valid not only for autopoiesis—the autocreation of the organic forms—but also for a healthy human relationship, for a prospering ecosystem as well as for an economy in harmony with the biospheric household.

These rules are the operational principles of the commons. They offer practical ways for commoners to build a new economy that is in greater alignment with natural systems—by limiting "externalities" that harm the rest of the ecosystem and other humans; by generating abundance for the larger whole; by providing a new vision for human development; and by fostering social and ecological exchanges that are enlivening. Any structure that tends to work according to commons principles is challenged by the double task of providing for the well-being of any individual without damaging the overarching whole. To find a universal framework for this is the task of the new culture that yearns to come alive.

Through a culture of enlivenment, an emancipation of a higher order becomes possible—just as the Enlightenment strived for liberation in a profound way. But the emancipation enlivenment aims at does not take its supplies from the promise of total sovereignty of the self alone, but is equally drawn from the desire for attachment. This "Enlightenment 2.0" no longer needs to separate theory from practice; the two can be constructively conflated, freeing us to build what can actually be built and to avoid chasing after totalistic, utopian theories. For utopia is everything that promises an unequivocal solution, everything that pledges to reduce the degree to which the things of this world are "dappled" (as Gerard Manley Hopkins put it)[13] and which claims to shrink the respective zone on the complex gradient between totality and isolation to an unambiguity that can be handled—and sold. Through this, utopia is an instrument of servitude.

If all things—matter and poetical gesture—are respectively tied to one another and to the unfathomable narratives of all others, then selling, the founding act of free markets, which attempts to establish unambiguity through the fiction of monetary value, is not only a moral flaw but a metaphysical mistake. It claims homogeneity where discontinuity reigns and needs to unfold its imaginative potential, which must not be controlled, in order to nourish the powers of life and of the soul. Money and market are instruments of an eliminative dualism that first encloses our soul and then annihilates it, by trying to enclose that which can never be controlled because even the instruments of domination are made from it: fertile life, which cannot be contained if it is not to direct its forces against itself.

5 COMMONS: INVITING THE OTHER

The enlivenment approach is not just an abstract philosophical reimagining of the world. It is an emerging reality in countless corners of the earth. The principles of enlivenment do not apply just to the living biosphere, or just to some archaic societies. They rather distinguish a wide variety of social innovations that are attempting to build a new sort of economy based on a personal practice that enhances participants' aliveness. These phenomena can be seen in highly diverse contexts: traditional societies, indigenous cultures, Internet culture, urban spaces, land and water management, and many others. Self-organized communities of people are bypassing the neo-Darwinian and neoliberal model by inventing their own novel forms of self-provisioning and governance.

It should be no surprise that this highly eclectic, uncoordinated social transformation is emerging mostly from the fringes of the mainstream economy. It amounts to a real-time reinvention of economics and governance by living communities of practice. Theory is still trying to catch up with the phenomena, but it is clear enough that commons-based initiatives are enacting the principles of enlivenment with varying degrees of self-awareness. The emergent new forms are blending the interests of the individual and the whole, and of meaning and material production and exchange.

These enlivenment-based models are integrating the social and the natural. They are rediscovering sense-making through practical action. It is striking that many of these projects explicitly reject the roles and rituals of conventional economics and state bureaucracies. They also tend to rebuff the cultural ethic of consumerism and markets, and to affirmatively honor participation, openness, accountability, and a rough equality. In this commons-based economy, people are not "consumers" and "producers" whose roles are defined by goods bought and sold through market exchange. They are, instead, *commoners* who initiate, debate, deliberate, negotiate, and plan among themselves as part of the process of meeting their collective needs.

Since market players despise alternative provision schemes as unwelcome competition, commons-based alternatives tend to flourish mostly on the edges of the mainstream economy and in cultural backwaters. Enlivenment communities often thrive in precarious milieus of the global South, for example, where people with little money have little choice but to devise solutions outside of the bio-economic corporate market system. The older, neglected practices of commoning are often a viable if not enlivening alternative to the impersonal, predatory norms of the market economy.

It is important to note that, even though the market economy tends to obscure this hidden social economy, commons-based systems play a significant role in meeting people's needs. Only through the "care work" that goes on within the commons of the family, which does not show up in any financial account, can new members of the work force be brought up and educated.[1] An estimated two billion people in the world depend on commons of forests, fisheries, water, farmland, wild game, and other resources for their everyday subsistence.[2] One could even argue that social norms, such as the regular greeting of others or the rules of politeness (not taking the last cookie), are rudimentary principles of the commons of a shared and cocreated world, in which everything belongs to everyone and nothing to only one person alone.[3]

In addition, huge segments of the software and computer industries revolve around open-source software platforms whose code is freely shareable and modifiable.[4] This infrastructure, in turn, hosts a complex global culture of digital commons that includes Wikipedia, collaborative websites, Creative Commons–licensed content, open access scholarly journals, and music remix and video mashup communities, among many others. The commons can also be seen in countless academic disciplines, community institutions, urban spaces, social activities, alternative currencies, and blood- and organ-donation systems. Despite all this, leading economics textbooks continue to ignore the commons as a functional alternative to current markets. As one commentator noted, mainstream opinion regards the commons as "no more than the institutional debris of societal arrangements that somehow fall outside modernity."[5]

An obvious reason why so many commons persist and flourish, even in our age of modernity, is because they are rich sources of personal, social, and even spiritual satisfaction. In their structure and operations, such enlivenment communities are focused not just on people-and-their-needs in a traditional economic sense—the production, distribution, and allocation of physical resources—but are also concerned with people's inner needs, their relationships to each other, and basic fairness and equality. The new provisioning forms generally attempt to bring individual interests and the whole into greater alignment as part of the process of meeting needs.

The animating forces of enlivenment economics are often invisible to conventional economists because the indicators of wealth creation—private property rights, legal contracts, money, market exchange—are missing. But enormous "wealth" is nonetheless being created through commons; it's just that the value generated is not usually monetized or wrapped in a legal envelope of property rights. The appeal of this hidden economy is not so strange. More and more people instinctively understand that the mainstream economy is deadening, whereas the commons-based economy—by fostering participation, personal initiative, social solidarity, and the like—helps people feel alive again.

The new approach to our physical and mental house-holding reveals that a subjective, felt, and experiential perspective is at the core of a true economics. Commons systems flourish in our sober times precisely because they are a source of personal, social, and spiritual satisfaction. Contemporary commons are less oriented toward the material needs of humans within the current understanding of economy (production, allocation, and distribution of resources through markets), but they focus on the inner needs of the participants, their relationships, fairness, and equality.

EXCHANGE OF PLENITUDE

These dimensions of the enlivenment economy raise a fundamental question that economists—by the very narrow definitions of their discourse—simply ignore, namely, "How can the economy be shaped to meet our needs and make us feel more alive?" Those two criteria are not entirely separate, after all. We might refine this line of inquiry further to ask: "What *are* our predominant needs here?" And "How can everybody's needs be met?" As we can easily see, such questions reflecting an enlivenment perspective are not only theoretical-philosophical, but always individual and concrete. They bring us deeply within the realm of the commons—or more accurately, of *commoning*, the everyday practice of managing a commons.

Commoning is the practical process of experience through which we can understand what needs are, and how they can be satisfied, beyond the market. Commoning is an attempt to redefine our very understanding of "the economy," which respectable opinion regards as a complicated machine driven by human automatons (*Homo economicus*) that requires constant oversight and correction by an anointed priesthood (economists). This is a dualistic, Enlightenment-style regime—one that pits business against customers, and the state against business (and business-as-state against humans). This sort of economy valorizes rationality over subjectivity, material wealth over human fulfillment, and the system's abstract necessities (growth, capital accumulation) over human needs.

The commons shatters these dualisms. It reconfigures our roles so that we are not simply "producers" and "consumers" with narrow economic, material interests, but participants in a physical and meaningful exchange with multiple material, social, and sense-making needs. Commoners realize that their household needs and livelihoods are entangled with their specific place and habitat, and with the Earth as a living being. They realize that their physical needs (hunger, thirst, health) are entwined with their search for existential meaning (a good life, joy, attachment). Finally, they realize that commoning, as an alternative system for meeting needs, is about a constant enactment and redefinition of a multitude of relationships, both material (metabolic) and psychological (symbolic).

An economic structure will thrive only if all of these dimensions are satisfied. This approximates the principles of the commons, in which our social and personal needs amalgamate with ecological complexities—a kind of integrated biospheric householding. Some examples can help illustrate these ideas. When villagers in India share seeds and use traditional farming practices, they are integrating their need for food with the natural cycles and features of the local ecosystem. This stands in stark contrast to a farming "economy" that looks to global prices, genetically engineered seeds, chemical pesticides and fertilizers, and monoculture crops—all of which are designed to monetize agricultural production and maximize returns to capital. That system appears to be highly "rational" in trying to organize structural efficiencies, but in truth it is deadening because it essentially turns individuals into mindless servants of a global economic machine. The system eliminates spaces for human agency and the meeting of embodied personal and social needs—the "vernacular spaces" in which humans can devise their own rules, express their own values, and negotiate preferred structures for meeting particular needs. One of the great underreported scandals of our time is how Western corporations have brought industrialized farming methods to rural India. More and more farmers fell into deep debt as they became dependent on proprietary seeds, volatile global markets, and corporate farming methods, among other factors. The result has been an epidemic of more than 300,000 farmer suicides in India since 1995.[6]

Commoning practices have attracted so much interest lately because they provide a direct and personal counterexperience to the inner emptiness of the prevailing bioeconomic model. The Newtonian, dualist bioeconomy has little room for local variation, custom, tradition, and ethical principles—all of which are irrelevant and extrinsic in a strict economic sense. In this way, the normal functioning of "the economy" strips away the very sense of meaning, belonging, and interpersonal commitments that define us as convivial, alive organisms.

BUEN VIVIR

In most regions of the world, corporate and national interests converge. Both reflexively seek to maximize economic advantages by eliminating whatever stands in their way. "Economic development" is taken as equivalent to human development. But in most cases, the economic gains accrue to a small elite group of investors, and any human development is a secondary and transient by-product. In the meantime, the many things that generate a sense of life and personal integration—smaller-scale enterprise, community traditions and stability, environmental beauty, social exchange, and belonging—are swept aside.

The point of commoning projects and the policies that support them is to restore enlivenment to the center of any economic activity. An economically sound project must also be an enlivening project. This means that it must try to reflect the shared interests of all and honor deeper human needs and the integrity of the natural surroundings.

The nations of Ecuador and Bolivia have tried to move in this direction by adopting provisions in their constitutions to protect *buen vivir*. As Bolivian writer Gustavo Soto Santiesteban explains, this concept, derived from the traditions of indigenous peoples, is aimed "at making visible and expressible aspects of reality that are ignored by the dominant paradigm. It is a proposal from a radical and spiritual perspective of ecology, and is logically incompatible with development and industrialization." Soto says that *buen vivir*

> implies several meanings manifested in community life: the fact of animals, persons and crops living together; living with Pachamama ("Mother Earth"—the water, the mountains, the biosphere) and finally, living together with the community of ancestors (*w'aka*). It is a community practice that finds organizational expression in the ... rural agricultural space where reciprocity predominates. It is evident that these enunciations are made from the commons, from the community, from the first-person plural, and not from "me," from the individual. Strictly speaking, the "individual" without community is bereft, orphaned, incomplete.[7]

Buen vivir is clearly aimed at fostering feelings that we all seek, like the feeling of being at home in a community or village or old-style city where most people know one another. Overcoming alienation and anonymity is probably the most important point of designing sustainable and common-economic projects.

It is easy to associate such aspirations with a premodern, preindustrial society, but in fact enlivenment is the "magic ingredient" for economic revitalization even in industrialized countries such as Germany. A recent survey for the German Federal Department for Building and Infrastructure[8] assessed the success of economic development projects launched in the failing, depopulated rural areas of eastern Germany. It turned out that the only truly flourishing projects were those that gave participants close personal connections with their communities and a sense of personal satisfaction. Economic turnaround required policies that foster enlivenment. The two are synergistic. The report to the German ministry concluded that any successful economic revitalization project must: (1) build on the natural assets of the environment while protecting their value; (2) build community by fostering social encounters, organizing traffic, and encouraging day-to-day livelihoods (schools, cafes, groceries, bakeries, etc.); and (3) promote bottom-up participation and innovation (i.e., the removal of external constraints that may prevent the community itself from deciding how to pursue change and spend monies). In locations that can no longer be exploited by the market economy, the principles of commoning and sharing economy are the only productive model.

Elinor Ostrom, who won the Nobel Prize in Economics in 2009 for her decades of theorizing and fieldwork study of commons, investigated how lobstermen in coastal Maine, communal landholders in Ethiopia, rubber tappers in the Amazon, and fishers in the Philippines could manage their shared resources sustainably without overexploiting them. She found that assuring maximal freedom on the local stage is a critical factor. Policymakers must not only give actors the opportunity to connect with one another and with their local environment, but give them the freedom to be creative and responsible. Local freedom is necessary to grant cohesion to the encompassing whole. We can express this empirical finding in terms of the enlivenment paradigm and its more specific maxims of (1) general principles but local rules; and (2) a balance of individuality and the whole (interbeing).

Local freedom is also one of the most cited advantages of markets—the unleashing of decentralized energies. But this trait is more often than not *thwarted* by the structural concentration of markets, in which large corporations and market oligopolies stifle local participation and innovation—a fact that has been observed many times.[9] Large market players make it their business to erect as many barriers to competition as may be legally permitted. In any case, markets are designed to maximize private gain and to "externalize costs" (displace them onto other people and the environment) as much as possible. By contrast, commons are under no compulsion to maximize economic output or privatize gains. With no structural imperative to be acquisitive or greedy, and every incentive to keep their local ecosystem sustainable and clean, commoners are more likely to be willing to support and advise fellow commoners.

BAREFOOT ECONOMY

Unlike market economics, commoning is not only about producing and distributing resources, but about constructing meaningful relationships with a place, with the Earth, and with one another. This is the hidden leverage power of commoning. Economists are not likely to see or understand these "invisible forces" because their vector of analysis is "rational" game theory and the workings of egoistic machines and selfish genes. The social, moral, and spiritual worlds of human existence have no real standing in standard economics. Yet these forces are precisely what bind together a commons, enabling it to function as a provisioning paradigm that is durable, effective, socially satisfying, and ecologically constructive.

For Donella Meadows, who spent her late life researching how to identify and define hidden leverage points for influencing systems that seem impervious to amendment, these feelings of enlivenment are an overlooked but profoundly influential trigger for real change.[10] Economic thinking in the existing paradigm is not likely to generate sustainable solutions because it is reluctant to recognize any meaningful role for self-organized human purpose and meaning in socioeconomic decision making. The purpose is always the same and always known in advance: unfettered economic growth. Therefore, even those who are desperately looking for change will typically overlook entirely feasible solutions and fail to catalyze systemic change because they are locked into a stunted worldview. Real solutions will not emerge unless actors first reframe their vision in a different paradigm.

Enlivenment can serve as a lever for change because it opens the door for commoners to do something completely "crazy"—that is, undertake a plan that is wholly unauthorized by a central, expert-driven model but that nevertheless makes absolute sense in human terms to real people on the ground, who reap immense personal satisfactions from honoring their intuitions, feelings, and firsthand knowledge.

This was precisely the origin of free software and open source software in the 1990s: programmers began to identify and solve coding problems that software companies had rejected as too trivial, ambitious, or simply unlikely to make money. Businesses must generally make serious investments and anticipate large returns before they can provide certain goods and services so that "risky" and "speculative" endeavors are avoided. But hackers operating as communities of shared practice could work on all sorts of important challenges that were deemed below the threshold of "rational" market action. They could freely "scratch their itch," as the hacker saying went, and trigger a whole cascade of socially driven collaborations resulting in useful software programs. No one functions as a producer or consumer, and the resulting program is not a "product." Everyone acts as "stewards" of the resource, and even the resource itself is more an element of the community itself than a separate, objective "other." This fits with the enlivenment principles by blurring the borders of "resource," "system," and "consumers." There is only one encompassing commons, which unfolds through the initiatives of a host of materially embodied actors.

This is particularly true for our participation in the abundance of nature. The same dynamic can be seen in countless commoners who engage with their nearby rivers, fisheries, wild game, forests, farmlands, and other resources. Their relationship is one of stewardship. The poet/farmer Wendell Berry contrasts this ethos with that of market culture, saying, "We know enough of our own history by now to be aware that people exploit what they have merely concluded to be of value, but they defend what they love."[11] Cultivating relationships with the more-than-human and with each other starts to create, as if out of thin air, new and mysterious leverage points for transforming systems in sustainable directions. But none of this is possible unless we can learn to rely on our embodied feelings as organisms and honor the communion with other humans.

It turns out that truly sustainable projects—sustainable in the long term—are always projects that satisfy the participants in a multidimensional way. They are projects that fulfill a richer scope of human needs that lie beyond the ostensible material, utilitarian self-interests of *Homo economicus*.[12] We can get a deeper understanding of these needs and their essential importance by looking at the matrix of human needs conceived by Chilean economist Manfred Max-Neef as a pivotal argument in his concept of barefoot economics. Max-Neef's goal was to design economic models that could meet the real needs of the poor of the global South who obviously do not profit from corporate capitalism.[13] This work amounts to a novel establishment of a first-person science (or in this case, a first-person economy) because it identifies embodied human needs that can be objectified and put into useful relationship to one another. Max-Neef's goal was to insert and integrate human needs into an economic theory, much as the commons does so in non-economic terms.

MAX-NEEF'S MATRIX OF HUMAN NEEDS

NEED	BEING (QUALITIES)	HAVING (THINGS)	DOING (ACTIONS)	INTERACTING (SETTINGS)
Subsistence	Physical and mental health	Food, shelter, work	Feed, clothe, rest, work	Living environment, social setting
Protection	Care, adaptability, autonomy	Social security, health systems, work	Cooperate, plan, take care of, help	Social environment, dwelling
Affection	Respect, sense of humor, generosity, sensuality	Friendships, family, relationships with nature	Share, take care of, make love, express emotions	Privacy, intimate spaces of togetherness
Understanding	Critical capacity, curiosity, intuition	Literature, teachers, policies, educational	Analyze, study, meditate, investigate	Schools, families, universities, communities
Participation	Receptiveness, dedication, sense of humor	Responsibilities, duties, work, rights	Cooperate, dissent, express opinions	Associations, parties, churches, neighborhoods
Leisure	Imagination, tranquility, spontaneity	Games, parties, peace of mind	Daydream, remember, relax, have fun	Landscapes, intimate spaces, places to be alone
Creation	Imagination, boldness, inventiveness, curiosity	Abilities, skills, work, techniques	Invent, build, design, work, compose, interpret	Spaces for expression, workshops, audiences
Identity	Sense of belonging, self-esteem, consistency	Language, religions, work, customs, values, norms	Get to know oneself, grow, commit oneself	Places one belongs to, everyday settings
Freedom	Autonomy, passion, self-esteem, open-mindedness	Equal rights	Dissent, choose, run risks, develop awareness	Anywhere

MATRIX OF HUMAN NEEDS

Max-Neef's matrix of human needs[14] is explicitly intended as a basic economic theory. His brilliant insight was to take economics at its word. It claims to be the science of allocation and distribution in order to satisfy human needs. So what *are* those needs? Max-Neef's framework of the economy clarifies that the range of our needs is much broader and richer than that set forth by bioeconomics, which explicitly eschews any substantive assessment of needs and collapses it into the single metric of utility. In the Darwinistic/neoliberal economic model, a human being (just like a corporation) is essentially a machine programmed to win and to kill as a strategy for surviving and prospering.

This programmed goal is *not* a need; a need can be interpreted, negotiated, postponed, or transformed with respect to other "players," which is precisely the enlivened freedom of any necessity. The goal of killing and absolutely winning and always behaving in such a way that the aim to win and to be better than others (also known as acting in "one's own interests") is attained not as the behavior of a living being, but as the behavior of a machine that is programmed in a linear fashion even if the actual programming consists of underlying mutually reflexive algorithms and cybernetic cascades. Machine behavior has no variability in relation to a change in its inner states and to variations in the environment or in the goals of other actors. This is why human behavior that mechanically clings to a certain goal or worldview and is not able to be reflected upon is called a personality disorder, such as narcissism. This is even its defining characteristic: personality disorders render behavior repetitive, machine-like, and unable to be influenced. We could thus say that bioeconomy leads to a narcissistic disorder of society.

Max-Neef's idea of a barefoot economy introduces new, empirical dimensions of need, meaning, and feeling into economic reasoning in a nontrivial and nonesoteric way. These analytic categories make legible some actual dimensions of human need that should influence our understanding of the emerging commons-based economy.

URBAN GARDENING

A trendy example of realizing objective benefits and at the same time experiencing subjective joy (or even "coolness") is the global urban gardening movement.[15] Within the last decade or so in major Western cities, a growing number of community gardens have arisen in many neighborhoods. Urban gardens act as a focus of health, communication, and multiethnic inclusion. They don't just cultivate high-quality food, they cultivate a new urban ethos—the idea that the city is not owned by corporate developers and defined by cars, concrete walls, and administrative orders. The city belongs to everybody.

Community gardens provide a real, physical space for people to realize new identities and to assert a modicum of autonomy over their lives and their food through cooperation and sharing. Once again, this ethic can arise only through subjects having experiences that in turn generates knowledge forged by practice. Urban gardening is about making a livelihood but also at the same time about learning the "gesture of the living" and, as Gregory Bateson put it, the "pattern that connects,"[16] because it is the way we communicate with ourselves, with other humans, and with anything alive.

Commons philosopher David Bollier states: "More people are starting to realize that public spaces like parks, community gardens, farmers' markets and festivals are also important to the economic and social health of a community. There is a dawning awareness that commons-based infrastructure like wireless Internet access is a great way to use a public resource, the airwaves, to help people connect with each other. ... The emerging commons sector provides benefits that corporations can't provide such as healthy ecosystems, economic security, stronger communities and a participatory culture."[17]

Keeping in mind Bateson's idea of enlivened structures as being expressive of "the pattern that connects," it is useful to see urban gardens and other commons-based innovations as a type of "pattern language," a term introduced by architect and artist Christopher Alexander. His basic idea is that living reality always follows a pattern language expressive of embodied existential needs that cluster in "centers of life." Anything that enhances aliveness is organized into meaningful patterns that we can readily discern and that offer satisfaction for us—for the simple reason that we are also alive.[18] Alexander argued that this is also a fundamental principle in the arts and in nature itself.

Alexander goes on to propose that any design that has living meaning—from architecture to political structure to urban design—should try to identify and embody the language of existential-aesthetic patterns. These patterns emerge as living beings experiment and consolidate their knowledge about what works and what doesn't, what is pleasing and enlivening and what isn't. The world is shot through with pattern languages that embody and express the sensual commons of the world, Alexander suggests. He more or less compiles a list of hidden principles of the commons, proposing, for example, that we "organize the planet as a commonwealth of independent regions."[19]

The identification of patterns-for-meaningful-aliveness dissolves the separation of practice and theory because the theoretical "plan" must always be lived and felt to be understood as relevant. Commoning exchanges are not meant to be fully theorizable, because much of their functioning comes from the contagious energy and feeling of one's own aliveness as it is being experienced and practiced. This is in line with my proposal to develop a first-person science that embraces both empirical subjectivity and poetic objectivity, as described above.

Commoning follows certain patterns of enlivening entanglement among human agents and their habitat—while fulfilling the material and inner needs of both. Meeting needs, building community, experiencing aesthetic pleasure and joy—all are combined in the single paradigm of commoning. One might say that commons are universal building blocks that can be used as centers of aliveness.

THE PLAY OF LIFE

These examples show that the shift from a neo-Darwinian/neoliberal economy to a world of biospheric householding is not a utopian dream.[20] It is happening now. It is the subject of a burgeoning academic literature and activist initiatives and policy proposals.[21] The common goal of so many of these efforts is to design human exchange circles that entail new, more fully human ways for people to relate to one another and to the more-than-human world. The goal is to foster more hospitable contexts for human sense-making so that humans can become productive participants in the nourishing cycles of the biosphere, and not be mere bystanders or exploiters of it (i.e., producers and consumers). Being an active participant in the biosphere does not mean obeying all its laws, but enacting freedom within the constraints of existential and ecological necessity.

For the German philosopher and poet Friedrich Schiller, the paradox of equally fulfilling our need to belong and our need to be autonomous is the culmination of culture. In his concept of aesthetic education, Schiller expressed his conviction that a negotiation of these paradoxes was necessary to live a true and meaningful life, a life that fulfills its potential and at the same time reveals the aliveness of the larger whole, and in this sense is aesthetic or poetic.

To resolve this paradox, Schiller did not choose the solution that Hegel (and in his wake, Marx and Engels) opted for a little later in history—to dissolve the contradictions in a "higher synthesis." Hegel and his followers aspired to actualize a supposed world-spirit and achieve a classless society whereby any human suffering could always be blamed on failing to get the dialectics right. Schiller, however, decided to stick close to the practice of the living, and in particular to the profound lessons learned in early childhood.

For Schiller, the entanglement of individual autonomy and larger necessity could be fulfilled only through play. Play unfolds from a person's free choice about *how* to do what is necessary. We are fully human only in play, Schiller believed. We are natural only in play, one might add.[22] It is not entirely fanciful to suggest that the practice of an enlivened economy amounts to nothing less than the practice of a rich and playful life. That vision, the deep attraction and satisfaction of serious play, may be the most potent, imaginative force for helping us deal with the realities of our time.

In this sense, the wisdom offered by Transition movement founder Rob Hopkins seems entirely applicable to the poetic practice of the enlivenment: "If it's not fun, you're not doing it right."[23]

6 POETIC OBJECTIVITY: UNDERSTANDING AS BEING FULLY ALIVE

For the last four hundred or so years, science has relied on an "objectivity" provided by rational thinking and technical measurements. The empirical method introduced by the British philosopher Francis Bacon had done away with scholastic speculation even though empiricism retained its discursive method of communicating through arguments. But the "objective science" that resulted is incomplete, because it fails to take into account the subjectively given reality of embodied selves.

If it is to become more reliable and insightful, science needs to go a step further and include shared embodied experience in its methodology. It should continue to rely on third-person "objective" methods of empirical observation and intellectual reasoning, but it must also introduce irreducible subjective meaning as a necessary element. Scientific thinking must develop a first-person account of its objects through its subjects. Science needs to incorporate poetic objectivity.

This may sound oxymoronic—how can science be both objective and subjective? But in fact subjective experience can be developed in a systematic way. Unhindered by conventions, bias, and jargon we can train our empiricism and communication to access those parts of ourselves and others to study and report on the living self. Poetic language allows us to systematically express our relationship with the world and with one another.

If we want to establish a scientific practice that derives its objectivity from its universal validity for all beings, we need to revalue our subjective experience and develop it farther. To be able to do so it is necessary to grasp the century-old heritage of mental enclosure. We need to open our eyes to the anesthesia that numbs the lives of humans already in their youth and which is cemented by educational systems still following the ideal of empirical-rational science formulated by Bacon in the early seventeenth century.

It is essential that we regain our fundamental right to express our own feelings in our relationships of householding and in our self-perception. The dualist perspective holds that we cannot know ourselves because mind and experience are incommensurate with matter, of which we are made. In this light, my suggestion does not seem to be very promising. But if we start with the finding that lived experiences are the common denominator for all embodied selves, from single cells on up, if we admit that these experiences are not inaccessible to the mind but rather are its foundation, then a deeper connection seems very much possible. We just have to rotate our point of view: the "ground of being"—the shared aliveness in a fertile cosmos—is not an unreachable enigma, the taboo of serious thinking, but the proper precondition for understanding.

There is one huge obstacle: many humans do not have good access to their proper needs on an emotional level.[1]

Needs, however, are nothing other than species-specific manifestations of that which we require as organisms, as productive subjects-in-connection, in order to flourish. Needs are individually distinct, but common to all. We all desire. We all crave connection, food, shelter, health, and freedom of choice—not only we humans, but also we animals and we beings. These needs do not mean anything else but that we are alive.

Existential needs manifest in feelings. Feelings cannot be switched off because they are reality. They don't go away. You can only lock them up. If feelings are locked up they become toxic. The pain of repressing one's own truth unconsciously legitimates the subjugation of others. This dilemma might be most deeply responsible for our incapability to transform our societies into more fertile cultures of reciprocity. We can observe the detachment from reality that ensues from disregarding real needs on several levels. It acts on the level of individual mental health, leading to pain in relationships between partners and between parents and children. But it also works on a larger scale within our society and in society's relation with the nonhuman world. We are acting out our pain of being enclosed on the level of our soul against the other beings who are not, who naively cling to the grace of their being just what they are.

It is therefore necessary to value our feelings in a completely new way. Feeling needs to be in the center of a culture of life, as it is our connection with the remainder of the world. We do not share our way of reasoning with other beings, but we all take part in the same way of feeling. We all are vulnerable beings who know the bitterness of pain and the sweetness of the self in ascent. To revalue feeling as an instrument of knowledge is a formidable task, as our civilization has been agreeing for centuries that feeling has no business at all in any serious matter of reality. By doing this, we have forsaken our most reliable organ of perception.

Feeling is true nonverbal knowledge. Through feeling, we dwell on this side of the polarity of things between mere weight and pure meaning. Feeling, therefore, is an instrument of perception. It is our most objective sensor for what is going on. But in order to really believe in this objectivity, we have to accept the basic premise of enlivenment—the fact that this world is not a collection of dead things of which some (humans and companion dogs, say) are imbued with consciousness for some mysterious reason, but instead that our reality is a vast poetic space: oneness, yearning to unfold and to know itself through fission and diversion.

If we want to start to rely on the objectivity of feeling, we have to accept that this cosmos is matter with a meaningful interior. Matter with a meaningful interior is the trait of something we intimately know, from the inside, as it is: life. We have to accept that this cosmos is alive. Then feeling becomes the deepest insight into the character of reality. Our own feeling reveals what happens to the world all the time: inwardness unfolding according to what happens to an exterior, a vulnerable and fragile assemblage of stuff—our body—happens to take on in a world made of light and shadow.

OBJECTIVITY AS THE ABILITY TO BE TOUCHED

To be alive is to be full of life. To be full of life includes not only the body, but also subjective experience. To allow ourselves to be full of life, we need a practice of aliveness that goes beyond the abstract objectivity of reason and incorporates the reality of the living organism and its proper emotions. Such an attitude understands reality as a network of relationships, takes the body seriously as the site of existential experiences, and no longer represses needs in the service of control and one's own functioning in accordance with the norms of others. This attitude is necessary for philosophy as a practice of our relationship with reality as well as for our daily practice of particular relationships, among friends and family as well as in the boardrooms of corporations.

The objectivity claimed by this attitude does not convey control, but is built from the courage to let go. For this reason, only this standpoint can be poetic. Poetic objectivity is not esoteric thinking. It is firmly anchored in reality. This reality, however, is not a place of value-free measuring and counting, but of embodied self-interests. Poetic objectivity is founded on empirical subjectivity. We all are subjects, but we can be subjects only through and with one another. We can be subjective only through being objective. Being a body is an irreducible fact *and* experience. We *are* bodies; we do not *have* bodies (which means that our body is a thing outside the self). We are bodies through a shared metabolism, through unconsciously partaking in the commons of light, air, and water. We *are* because we are with-others. As subjects-together we can negotiate a fertile perspective toward aliveness. This is the true objectivity life is capable of. This insight challenges Descartes's old dogma that we can only be sure about our mind (*Cogito ergo sum*).[2]

You can gain subjective certainty about your body and your experience, which is a certainty in the first person. The first-person perspective of this experience already includes the other in order to establish self and the feeling of oneself. The ensuing certainty is not the neutrality of a detached spectator, but a deep entanglement of the matters of the world and one's own self. The resulting knowledge is a feeling of certainty about one's own needs and about the degree to which we succeed in entering into connection with others. Even Descartes's famous dictum can be traced back to this certainty (although he would not have admitted it). It is a statement made by a being of flesh and blood, even though it presumes to be in league with divine objectivity and therefore more powerful.

Enlivenment works through accepting body not as a "grave" and deplorable restriction of freedom, but as the condition of the possibility of freedom. To be a body, to be a self with emotions, and to continuously transmute by means of verbal and nonverbal interactions is the empirical desire of beings. It shapes the preconditions and the patterns of subjective and existential experience. Poetic objectivity relates to the subjective core self: the existential meaning any organic being produces from that center of concern that is its self.

The crucial point is that we all—all of us living beings, from the most modest bacterial cell in our guts to you, the reader—share the experience of a meaningful core self that is concerned with what happens to it and strives to keep itself alive. As living beings, we all have a genuine interest in continuing to live, and we know the joy and light-footed exuberance of just being. Poetic objectivity seeks to understand how expressiveness-in-our-body feels and can be communicated and elaborated upon. It desires to be a response to the expressive power of the body, and it strives to be communicated and refined. In the self-experience as joy lies the key to the connection between matter and sense, the unspeakable kinship of being and meaning which can never be fully understood, which can only be participated in.[3]

This poetic gesture is the natural expression of experiences in an existence that is expressive-embodied from the start. This gesture is answered by artists: a work of art seizes us emotionally and thus shows us something profound about aliveness. This emotional understanding is a shared existential experience—a poetic objectivity. It is not fundamentally different from experiences that we make while meeting other beings in "nature." Every organism is a poetic expression of life. It is totally closed in itself and absolutely transparent.

Poetic objectivity is not the objectivity of a scientist's proof. Scientific objectivity exercises imperial rule by excluding the subjectivity of living beings, which in truth is a crucial feature of the world. Poetic objectivity does not attempt to prevail. Poetic objectivity is deliberately weak. We cannot "prove" it with quantification or controlled, reproducible experiments. We can only try to bring it to the observer and let it do its work by transmitting the gift of life, by arousing the desire for aliveness. In this sense, poetic objectivity has more power than any scientific reasoning because we can feel it and because it can transform our actions even before our conscious minds can recognize it. Great literature is able to transform a personal life, as is the experience of nature and the presence of other beings. Insights can be won not only by one's own experience, but also by experiencing crystallized poetic experience.

The philosopher Ivy Campbell-Fisher observed: "If I could be as sad as some passages in Mozart, my glory would be greater as it is. ... My grasp of the essence of sadness comes not from moments I have been sad, but from moments when I have seen sadness before me released from entanglements with contingency ... in the works of our great artists."[4] Poetic objectivity provides not an empirical but an embodied proof. It is a validation of the processes by which the individual creates itself through the whole, which can only be participated in through emotional involvement.

THINKING LIKE A MOUNTAIN

Poetic objectivity requires that we can submit any practice to the questions: Is this productive imagination? Is this exchange between self and other? Does it provide grace? Does it enhance aliveness? Does it bring more life? Do I make life fuller? These are obviously not the same questions utilitarians ask when they are looking for maximal benefit (a proxy metric for the common good). From an enlivenment approach, questions about the common good point in a different direction and rely on qualitative judgments. They take individual experience, freedom, growth, and health into account and recognize that any life-enhancing improvement can be grasped only by poetic imagination. It cannot be analyzed or directly measured. It can be known solely through experience—in the same way that the truth of a poem can only be understood from within the core self of a sentient being who uses language as a means of understanding the self of another being. Poetic objectivity is objectivity only because it is shared. It is objective from a shared perspective in the first person.

The idea of poetic objectivity, which transforms the inanimate "view from the outside" (empirical rationality) into an experience from within (empirical subjectivity), calls for a first-person science to generalize this richer kind of knowledge. To be clear: a first-person approach is not equivalent to the human ego perspective. Rather, it gives voice to feelings that are repressed by the controlling human ego, as well as to the first-person experiences of other beings. A first-person science would also take into account the inner dimensions of foxes and fish, rivers and forests, oceans and shores.

This experience cannot be fathomed in an erudite essay alone. To take such a perspective is, as the pioneering ecophilosopher Aldo Leopold described it, to "think like a mountain."[5] To think like a mountain does not mean thinking from the standpoint of the individual, but from the creative and productive way of life; only in this way can we understand what lies beyond our limited imagination. This space beyond is the objectivity of poetic knowledge. It cannot be extracted, but is accessible only by careful participation, by offering its own life to be populated by the lives of others. "Only the mountain has lived long enough to listen objectively to the howl of a wolf," writes Leopold.

This objectivity is an accurate description, but it is also an attitude. We have an opportunity to come into contact with the nobility of being if we expose ourselves to the perspective of the whole biosphere and do not give in only to our needs for sovereignty and protection. The nobility of being is what in this world is most vulnerable and at the same time most difficult to eradicate. The insurgence against controlling objectivity defends this nobility against the banality of the attitude of seeking rescue only for oneself. This defense is also to think like a mountain. Or like a marsh in autumn. Leopold writes: "Amid the endless mediocrity of the commonplace, a crane marsh holds a paleontological patent of nobility, won in the march of aeons, and revocable only by shotgun."[6]

One of the deep limitations of conventional scientific objectivity is its inability even to depict the need for social justice, or a fairer economy, or a sustainable climate, because it by definition excludes the first-person perspective of other beings. Poetic objectivity helps us overcome this problem by enabling us to rethink our relationship with the Earth. It lets us feel our relationship with the Earth in a new way. It allows us to properly recognize human life as a matter of embodied living within the biosphere, blending materiality and meaning in one huge commons of atoms, thoughts, and desires.

Using this lens, we can reintegrate the material, or third-person, aspect of reality with the felt, first-person side of the equation that is otherwise "hidden within." This first person encounters the world as a "thou." Both are equally valid and cannot exist alone without distorting our understanding of the full context. The American poet and ecophilosopher Gary Snyder nicely expresses this relation with a short, koan-like passage in one of his major poems:

As the crickets' soft autumn hum

is to us

so are we to the trees

as are they

to the rocks and the hills.[7]

Born from a moment of attachment that cannot be repeated, any careful poetic description of a phenomenon of life becomes a scientific observation. A beautiful example of ecological research in the first person is the poetic genre of nature writing as represented by John Muir, Barry Lopez, Gary Snyder, David Abram, Robert Macfarlane, and others.[8] In the fine arts, the eco-art movement has been experimenting with first-person scientific perspectives on our aliveness for decades, producing a host of highly interesting insights that nonetheless cannot be easily translated into verbal descriptions.[9] From the standpoint of this essay, these are all scientific explorations in a shared living world. They are poetic practices of perception, practices of the respective individual transformations that come about through being attached to others and to the world.

The call for poetic objectivity does not mean proposing an entirely individualistic or solipsistic worldview. Nor does it argue for more effusion. Rather, the subjective perspective of embodied beings is a necessary complement to the prevailing objective approach. The metabolizing body in its subjective desire transforms matter into imagination, not randomly, but following the principles of living relationships.

This is what the Berlin-based philosopher Armen Avanessian calls "speculative poetics": an imaginative practice that creates a world ever anew by trying to impregnate it. Avanessian holds that our experience is centered not around "epistemes" (concepts of knowledge), but around "existemes" (categories of experience). These existemes provide at the same time unprecedented imagination and binding norms which are valid at all times. We could say the same about natural history.[10]

As living organisms, we have to learn to experience and to describe the world "from the inside" (emotionally, subjectively, socially) while also treating it as an external physical reality that exists "outside" of us. Bruno Latour has ingeniously explained that any procedure that attempts to "purify" the biosphere by insisting upon its physical dimensions—while denying that it is also a sphere of meaning, or "semiosphere"—will only generate even greater, albeit hidden, tensions that are all the more devastating the more deeply hidden they lie.[11] Here again we find a parallel with individual psychology: repressing hidden antagonisms leads to neurosis. Contradictions cannot be pushed aside but must be transformed by giving them living expression. To express contradictory needs is, however, to risk being vulnerable. We need to be willing to take that risk if we are to be alive.

SENTIENCE AS RESEARCH INSTRUMENT

The idea of poetic objectivity acknowledges that our vulnerability is a scientific instrument. Many people may object that such an idea stretches the definition of science to a breaking point, because the notions of measurement, reproducibility, and falsifiability have traditionally been seen as key elements of the scientific method. The idea of poetic objectivity makes the case—boldly and frankly—for a broader, more reliable scientific methodology that respects the inwardness that comes with the reality of life.

A first-person science should attempt to corroborate those theoretical findings with methods that make felt existence accessible to others and enable the sharing of these experiences. First-person science considers feeling, expressiveness, and meaning to be components of an important engine of scientific inquiry. Experiential methods are not the only tools, of course, but together with empirical observation and reasoning they provide means to refining and sharing our experiences. They can become objective in regard to the body, which is the common ground of experience in all organisms.

This type of science is not new. Many cultures from diverse epochs have developed techniques for providing a first-person account of ourselves within the world. We thus should be able to draw guidance from these traditions, many of which are still in use today or are being rediscovered. The rituals of indigenous cultures to which I have already referred above are fed by this source. But Western art also follows the principle of understanding reality from one's own living existence at a particular spot between totality of the whole and the separation of the individual. Henry Miller had in mind this notion that art is a means to accessing knowledge about life, when he said: "Art teaches nothing, except the significance of life."[12] We can view art as a means of inquiry into the world, which relies on the sentient and vulnerable body as a means of revelation of insight—a poetic insight, not a causal-objective one, an insight following the understanding that "men are grass."

Science itself probes into this practice of experience in the first person. The neurobiologist Francisco Varela explicitly tried to unite empirical brain research, Buddhist meditation, and phenomenological insight into a first-person science.[13] In his later work, Varela complemented brain-imaging techniques with a careful questioning of how the research subject felt and what he or she experienced. Varela regarded meditation as a scientific method of understanding the self in the world, and the self as a world, which cannot simply be marginalized as personal, subjective experience.[14] He found that the feelings of serene emptiness elicited by meditation complement the scientific finding that organisms exist without a fixed anchor of identity, but rather as living beings implicated in a "meshwork of selfless selves."[15]

Another traditional example of a first-person method of sharing embodied insight is the Native American "medicine wheel" methodology common among the American First Nations. The medicine-wheel ritual creates a cosmic space, a setting among the more-than-human world that is at the same time an emotional and symbolic space. It enables a visualization of one's own self in a gestural and poetic way as being part of the self-containing nature, putting oneself into contact with the presence of other beings, and thereby allowing for the reality of one's own feelings. Through this constellation, insights emerge that the attitude of control otherwise easily blocks.

Inspired by ways of the American First Nations to enact the human role in a cosmos that requires reciprocity and the culture of the gift, the US nature philosopher and wilderness educator Jon Young has developed a rich, modern methodology to cultivate a mentoring style that brings back the indigenous attitude of being part of a fertile cosmos that is thoroughly alive. The goal is to enable practitioners to develop their feelings through contact with other sentient beings. This is a way to experience one's own sensitivity and vulnerability in contact with the real.[16]

ROMANTICISM 2.0

Romanticism has been a perennial stronghold for poetic science research. Romantic thinkers have sketched out several explicit programs for poetic objectivity: Novalis and Johann Gottfried Herder, among others, in the German-speaking world; in the British "Northern Renaissance," Samuel Taylor Coleridge and William Wordsworth; and, later, in the United States, Ralph Waldo Emerson and Henry David Thoreau. At the end of the eighteenth century in Germany, young Romantic thinkers, among them presumably Friedrich Hölderlin and Friedrich Schelling, formulated a research program that culminated in the idea that a precise description of the world could possibly be given only "in a language of poetry, in a language of love."[17] This language automatically includes other beings as referents for emotions and metaphorical self-understanding.

We can find the idea of a first-person natural history, which expands the notion of the observer's poetic involvement in the role played by the exact scientist, in the works of Alexander von Humboldt, Johann Wolfgang von Goethe, and Friedrich Schiller. The major aesthetic theories of Goethe and Schiller both follow this Romantic approach. Goethe's position is especially interesting: he is mainly known for his achievements as a poet, but he himself thought his scientific activities to be more valuable. Goethe did not reject the scientific method, but tried to complement it with the "delicate empiricism" of a more poetic and involved approach. Goethe thought of nature as a grand process of artistic revelation—and also believed that a successful work of art must represent nature's creative forces to some degree.

The British literary scholar Elizabeth Sewell has shown that this school of thought tried to explain how "the orphic voice" of a deep poetic expressivity permeates all reality.[18] Romanticism has left us with a host of questions we still have not even touched on. The relationship between the interior (experience, emotions, mind) and nature (matter), which was the centrifugal point of Romantic thinking, has still not been solved. This question has instead become a forbidden terrain that we mostly ignore. To my mind, the conviction that we have to push aside the questions that intrigued the Romanticists contributes to the factors leading to the dilemmas posed by the ongoing global crisis.

In one sense, we could call the enlivenment approach "Romanticism 2.0." Romanticism was the search to understand the fertile character of the world through its appearances. It followed the claim that "phenomena" are not to be shoved aside as mere illusions but that they convey a poetic knowledge through which the world expresses itself. Romanticism is fairly modest concerning the human ability to understand the cosmos as being something separate. The world's interior is forever ungraspable as totality. But it can be approached and embraced as individuality. Its interior permeates the uncountable permutations of the surface of things, which in turn become the sensitive skin of a vulnerable flesh. This flesh vibrates with a continuous desire to be touched, to touch, and to make itself feel. The world is sentience *because* it is matter.

The mission of Romantic thinking has not been made obsolete by scientific progress. If anything, it is needed more today than it was over two hundred years ago. The issues the Romantics were concerned with have been pushed aside without due regard for the profound epistemological errors that this omission has introduced. Many of our current difficulties stem from the fact that we rejected the Romantic notion of the world as something that is inherently creative and alive (despite the fact that we feel we are alive in every moment) and then proceeded to build an entire civilization upon this flawed foundation.

We should realize that Romanticism was not about (or at least not only about) the elevation to artistic dignity of wild emotions, subjective feelings, gruesome experiences, and personal suffering. It was first and foremost a scientific way of exploring the world as a subjective phenomenon. The first generation of Romantics in Germany and England (Coleridge, Hölderlin) were motivated by understanding how matter can be expressive of inwardness. They set out to build a first-person science, which remains incomplete.

Hölderlin understood this endeavor as the "need for a new mythology."[19] His notion was that the world itself is a poetic space that creates the desire for unity through its inherent differentiations. Poetry is the manifestation of the human capability to be part of the world, and to partake in its fertility. Romanticism's original intuition about a disjunctive unity of a material world, however, was eroded by a stream of thought that paid more attention to the creative powers of the subject-mind. This eventually became the idealism of Fichte and Hegel, which buried the original

Romantic endeavor under an avalanche of subject-obsessed artistic and philosophical output, and ultimately produced the strong notion of the lonely subject, uncoupled from reality, arbitrarily constructing its world. In comparison to the fate of the movement in Germany, the British Romantic "Northern Renaissance" was a little more successful in conserving the original quest for a language of meaning to be found in nature. This heritage has stayed alive until today through the comparatively late American Romanticism and Transcendentalism.

Unlike eighteenth- or nineteenth-century thinkers, however, we can reevaluate the original Romantic idea in light of the extensive recent findings of advanced biology, systems research, biosemiotics, and quantum physics. All of these sciences now validate the original Romantic claim that the living world's principles can be seen in the appearances of living bodies and meadows, streams and forests. In imagining ourselves and the world in fertile reciprocity, we are able to bring to life the principles of a living world. There is reason to believe that this will not result in a "new mythology," however—it will not draw a new veil over the world, but instead give birth into a new enlightenment regarding our involvement with the world.

The German artist Joseph Beuys revived the Romantic heritage in the philosophy guiding his work. He drew heavily from Goethe and his integrative understanding of creative processes, leading to an entanglement of life and art that is evident in its creativity and its productivity. Beuys spent his life trying to expand art into the general sphere of everyday activities—that (often-trivialized) notion that "everybody is an artist." For Beuys, life processes can be understood and emulated only if they are perceived as being part of the unfolding creativity of a living self in contact with others. This attitude clearly brings to mind the notion of "poetic objectivity" developed above.

Beuys called his approach to changing reality through imagination the "warmth process" or "warmth work."[20] He believed that every gesture resulting from processes of life is inherently creative and productive. Conversely, this also means that only enlivening processes can truly transform society and one's own consciousness.

POETIC PRECISION

"There is no wealth but life," wrote the British nineteenth-century artist and philosopher John Ruskin. But what is the standard for assessing the wealth of life? Just as Enlightenment thinking has had its conspicuous shortcomings, so the proposed first-person science must be approached with healthy caution. It needs to be performed with tenderness, with what Goethe called "delicate empiricism."[21] Where objective science renders the world more and more lifeless through its tendency to dissect, analyze, and state half-truths, subjective science could easily degenerate into a system of unchecked irrationality and manipulations of the gullible.

The mere sense of "feeling alive" has no explanatory content whatsoever. A nice-sounding poem might be full of clichés. In group processes seeking to cultivate mindfulness, charismatic leaders may easily dominate and mislead others, a phenomenon referred to in the literature as the result of an "expanded ego." There is also the danger of seduction into emotional states that might feel quite poetic, but which have no basis in reality, and which cannot be truly shared.

We easily confound the overwhelming feeling of closeness and the experience of "being really alive" with psychological fusion and projection, which always carry with them some sorts of emotional abuse. "Coming to oneself" per se, then, is not a reliable basis for a first-person science. A mass murderer can feel alive when committing his crime; he probably does, and that is the reason for his behavior: his personality disorder makes him feel dead and disconnected at all other times. A fetish for feeling alive can in this way degrade into totalitarianism. This is the main reason why Western civilization has developed its scientific method: to safeguard against seduction and superstition by requiring testable, reproducible results. Empirical proofs are thought to be democratic.

But whereas empiricism reclaims the ostensible neutrality of science which must do away with individual feelings and experiences, poetic objectivity is based in a much higher scale on the consideration of the true needs of others and their vulnerable bodies. The key to avoiding an abuse of the first-person perspective through emotional contagion or plain toxic tyranny is the other: it is the other's flourishing that sets the limits on what I can freely do. It is not about me, but about the fertility of the whole, which includes myself.

Aliveness in its innermost core carries the plea that there be life, not that I am fine. Putting the desire that there be life first might even provoke my own destruction.[22]

It is therefore necessary to negotiate the antagonistic tendencies of lived reality, to become more vulnerable, to give, not to gain more. This idea of life as a constant letting go is the opposite of the esoteric cliché of a world where death is not real. If we accept nature as the epitome of freedom-in-necessity, we can no longer regard it as a haven of morally elevated, beautiful, and healthy behavior. Ecological thinking often tries to substitute a nostalgic, Mother Earth version of redemption for the deadening, rational dystopia of modern times. In truth, both options represent an evasion. They each set up an impossible utopia that is hostile toward life. To be really alive is to be embedded in a mess that must constantly be negotiated. This is the species-specific way *Homo sapiens* realizes its contradictions. It is the only way that culture can emerge.

More than anything, we need to nurture a culture of poetic precision, to be observant of felt life while accepting the material processes in the world. We must develop freedom within this framework of necessity. We must know passion but make decisions in an informed manner. We must cultivate an empathetic attitude but recognize that some suffering cannot be avoided. We must acknowledge death as the ultimate transformative power. We must know that existence has paradoxical traits: that every light casts a shadow, that each debauchery has to be paid, that connection—not fusion—is possible, that we have to face death on a personal level and on the civilizational plane, and that only by coping with these calamities is real transformation possible—if we counter them bravely in full acceptance, without wanting to abolish them.

BEING IS PERCEIVING

The most convincing guideline for a culture of poetic precision is to always put the other's needs first. This is to understand the other—streams and forests, bees and birds, children and lovers—as the source of one's own aliveness, and at the same time to understand that one's own being is a key to the other's existence. This ethos means accepting the "thou" as something unfathomable, which cannot be subject to judgment. The idea of an irreducible other who allows the individual to thrive by means of a continuous exchange is a key aspect to a philosophy of the commons.

This perspective is possible when the observer is able to see herself and others as embodied subjects with their own needs, and not just as objects for the fulfillment of self-serving desires. Opening oneself up to the other's aliveness makes possible the experience of "embodied interbeing." We realize that only through the mirror of the other can we become aware of ourselves. Empirically, this "other first" principle is how the world works anyway: on ecological grounds, we all come to be solely through others who feed us and upon whom we feed, and with whom we exchange oxygen and carbon, water, energy, shelter, and mutual bonds. The other is the indispensable partner who enables a human infant to grow into his humanity. Only if the caregiver really "sees" the baby and the baby's needs, and deeply welcomes these needs, can an infant develop a healthy, socially adjusted personality.

True subjectivity that is aware of its dependency on a mutual meshwork of life-giving relationships means seeing *through* the other. It puts the other first and gives him the instrument of one's own perception. The expanded vision of self-in-reciprocity builds on the wisdom that to exist always requires being perceived, and to perceive is to call into being. Self and other coexist in a mutually inclusive manner. Neither is possible alone. A self that is unsure of itself will fail to welcome the other. Failing to relate to the other is not a viable strategy for maintaining life. The aliveness of self is only possible because there already exists a separate "thou" that is able to give life, always feeding the network of reciprocal interdependence.

In this constellation, neither the ego, nor the other as source of absolute norms and laws representing a superego, stands in the center. The bond as such becomes the center of mutual transformation and joint imagination. The shared being grows into a curious, loving research of what can become. This broadened vision means truly thinking through the other. It is close to what Aldo Leopold described as "thinking like a mountain," which also can mean thinking ourselves through the mountain. Leopold suggested that we see with the mountain, adopt it as a sense organ, and that we experience the world from the standpoint of another individuation of this same world. "Seeing with a mountain" is the utmost degree of altruism: I consider the world from the perspective of the ecosystemic totality and not from the standpoint of my own world alone.

This does not mean eclipsing oneself in favor of a "higher self," however. On the contrary: seeing with the mountain, or thinking with it, frees the self from the restraints of a single focus of vision. It is therefore another means of poetic imagination. It is a weave in the flesh of the world. This way of reimagining oneself through living otherness evokes Paul Cézanne, the painter, who grasped through the mountain of his life, the Montagne Sainte Victoire, that "nature is on the inside"; he envisioned the other of this mountain through color and shape, in the form of a relationship in which he, the observer, was also reinvented.

7 CULTURE: IMAGINING THE OTHER

In the poem "Like a Countless Bird," the French Caribbean author and political philosopher Édouard Glissant unfolds a poetic epistemology that "attunes to the odyssey of the world. ... It is possible to approach this diverse chaos and to grow by the unforeseeable occasions it contains ... to pulsate with the pulsation of the world which is still to be discovered."[1] Glissant argues that we have to think in creative paradoxes that embrace their own opposites. This resonates quite strongly with the ecological poetics proposed here: we can only embrace the paradoxes of lived existence if we allow ourselves to think in an embodied fashion, as consciousness in physical form. To think in an embodied fashion is to feel. The language of first-person science is poetic.

Glissant calls his philosophy the "thinking of tremor." The tremor is terror, but at the same time it is our sole certainty, because only the cracks it leaves behind allow a connection to the outside. This attitude relies on the imaginative objectivity that comes from our vulnerability as an organ of perception. The thinking of tremor is *enlivenment*-in-action. Glissant's concept presupposes the painful connection between thought and feeling, experience and politics, local and global, that marks every experience of being in touch—an experience that can never be reduced to its building blocks.

Glissant's poetics is an illustration of the power of inviting contradictions into our worldview to allow us to exist and even flourish. It celebrates the richness of an existence that defines itself not by *identities*, but by *relationships*. Following Glissant, one should not speak of "my race" versus "others," "culture" versus "natural resources," or "feeling" versus "thinking"; we should instead be loyal to a destiny that binds all of this together in one struggle for identity. This struggle expresses itself in a particular biography that relates to a particular place that is a particular habitat for particular species—yet nonetheless has universal resonances. We must not fight these contradictions or flatten them out. They are the material of life's creativity and the raw stuff on which improvisation draws.

CULTURE AS AN ECOLOGY OF CONTRADICTIONS

Glissant's poetics show how the natural history of "dependent-freedom-in-incompatibility" can be integrated into a poetics of the world, and how this poetics lends itself to a political view of the world. In the center of this view stands the certainty that all lived reality, be it physiological, ecological, emotional, sociological, political, economic, or artistic, is paradoxical—and precisely because it is paradoxical is it life-giving.

Glissant argues for a "poetics of diversity."[2] Drawing on his African-Caribbean background, he calls his search for productive contradictions a "creolization of thought." We have to accept the absoluteness of the total and the individual at the same time; we have to see that identities are existential but only brought about momentarily, through the interbeing of relations. We could say that Glissant's concept of a creolization of thought, which relies so much on the admission of contradictions, is also an ecologization of thought. Ecology, then, can be understood as the description of a relational whole composed of individuals who thrive on their incompatibilities. Individuals can be nourished by the whole only if they remain vulnerable, touchable—indeed, edible. Glissant's "thinking of tremor" therefore is also the "thinking of life."

As the expression of continuous transformational processes and ongoing self-creation, ecological systems—with humankind in their midst—are sliding from catastrophe to catastrophe. Already the mere living cell is self-contradictory. Its existence results from the interplay of two entirely different forms of coding in our bodies, the abstract-genetic-binary and the felt-somatic-analogous. Only by being incompatible and by needing continuous translation can these two code systems together generate meaning and hence coherence.[3]

Lived reality is self-contradictory—and every culture managing to enliven this reality must also be contradictory—albeit poetically so—to some extent. Perception partakes in this dimension of nature's commons by admitting the contradictions of the poetic. A grazing commons in some remote highland is an ecological and economic paradox, because only by strictly forbidding the usage of the pasture at certain times can this resource be preserved and remain available in the future. On the other hand, the growing grass needs to be fed upon; the resource must be used if it isn't to perish. It needs to be annihilated on a regular basis; otherwise it will gradually become a forest. And the same is true even for poetry: a poem needs the "blessed wound" of misunderstanding in order to allow for the transformation of the written words into imagination.[4]

From this viewpoint, the inner ecology of the cell and the social ecology of humans seem to be mere levels in a continuous interplay of freedom and necessities. The living world, Glissant argues, is self-contradictory because it is "a world in which all human beings and animals and landscapes and cultures and spiritualities illuminate each other. But illumination is not dilution."[5] The worldview based on these creative contradictions could be called "biopoetics"—in contrast to the prevailing perspective of "bioeconomics."[6]

CULTURE AS ANTI-UTOPIA

The essential stance of a biopoetic point of view is that we must cultivate living contradictions. This is important not only if we wish to recognize paradoxes as paradoxes, but also if we are to find in them the deep root of an enlivened spirit. That means that we have to accept death as an integral part of life—even as life's decisive precondition and most intimate mirror image. Death is a prerequisite for development.

It is necessary to take a closer look at the dialectics of death. Above I observed that by reducing the living world to nonliving building blocks, the prevailing scientific approach has evolved into an "ideology of death." If we accept the ruling assumption that, in fact, the world is nonliving, the experience of lived reality has no real value. Paradoxically, this attitude is bolstered by the attempt to control the world and to improve on its flaws—namely, by the attempt to work toward a better human life. In emphatically striving for life, bioeconomics does not accept death as a reality within life and therefore becomes a practice of the nonliving. It creates death, because it does not accept the reality of death as part of a fertile life that desires to produce birth.

We can only value aliveness if we admit its intimate connection with dying. All organisms engage in a constant struggle with the forces of dead matter. On such a perspective, death is an integral part of life, and only through it can life flourish. Only by accepting nonbeing, failure, temporal limitation, and the fact that every process will come to an end can we empower the creativity needed to bring forth growth and newness.

Life processes make for incomplete creations, because creation cannot be anything but flawed. To strive for perfection rather than connection is to position oneself outside creation. It is an attempt to control aliveness, an attempt that inevitably produces death. The truly utopian power we retain in this situation is nothing we have to fight for, because it is already there as a choice offered to us. It is imagining something new within the restraints of the factual, the "rejoicing of the possible" (according to Martin Buber) in the lived necessity of the moment. It is the transparency of aliveness in the opacity of life, never to be cashed in as empirical facts, but always present.

Seen from this angle, life is, as the author and scholar Natalie Knapp puts it, "a complete disaster."[7] Anyone who pretends otherwise is just sweeping the matter under the carpet. Mindfulness pioneer Jon Kabat-Zinn proposes "full catastrophe living."[8] No concept, philosophy, or ideology will change this situation, because the precarious and disastrous nature of any living organization results from its being an expression of the underlying desire of the whole to reconnect through the clefts of its own differentiation, which are needed if any connection is to be possible. Any process is in reality an incomplete attempt at translation—a bridging of two incompatible but mutually translatable domains. And translation is poetry.

Death co-constructs this edifice. Without it, there is no life. The disconcerting implication of this insight is that we must systematically include incompleteness in our search for fertility. Incompleteness, in experiential terms, is vulnerability, and the pain that follows it is unavoidable. Fertility thus needs to cope with indeterminacy and emotional disaster, if it is to develop into joy.

For all these reasons, a culture of life is emphatically anti-utopian. It refrains from any illusions, metaphysical "success stories" (as Hans Jonas puts it),[9] or offerings of mental appeasement and satisfaction. But to be anti-utopian is not to be dystopian. It does not mean giving up the quest for an enlivened reality. On the contrary, it means only that this quest is, by its very nature, endless, never to be completely achieved, which is not to say that it won't offer results and rewards.

If living beings necessarily exist in a world of paradox, we must start seeing the contradictory dimensions of life as complementary and not try to resolve them. It means that we must *use* nature and at the same time *protect* it through the way we use it (the way large herbivores protect savannas by grazing on it, for example). It means that we see economic exchange as suffused with emotional bonds. It means accepting pain and death as necessary complements of any enlivening growth process, and not trying to deny or repress them as our hedonistic culture typically does. Enlivenment means accepting that to remain the same, we may need constant, often painful transformation. It means, finally, that feeling enlivened does not necessarily mean feeling good.

This is what Vaclav Havel had in mind when, during his life as a dissident and Samizdat writer in former socialist Czechoslovakia, he noted: "Hope is definitely not the same thing as optimism. It is not the conviction that something will turn out well, but the certainty that something makes sense, regardless of how it turns out."[10] The quest for enlivenment is possible only if we are aware that we will never achieve a complete victory against imperfect but improvable conditions.

As a civilization, we should stop chasing after victories, and instead invest in the appreciation of the fragile moment. We should more behave the way a young dog does, or a mining bee doggedly following the inner aims of its existence. We should devote ourselves to the bliss and the sadness of the imperfect now. That means to start accepting and knowing ourselves. It means admitting one's own sentient wildness, and through this acceptance, granting all others their space. This is what Gary Snyder recommends as well when he observes: "The Grizzlies or Whales or Rhesus Monkeys, or Rattus, would infinitely prefer that humans (especially Euro-Americans) got to know themselves thoroughly before presuming to do Ursine or Cetacean Research."[11]

CULTURE AS EMOTIONAL ENGAGEMENT

The creolization of thinking to which Edouard Glissant refers requires "peership" between empirical reality and feeling.[12] All processes take place inside and outside an organism simultaneously. They are always conceptual and spiritual, but they are also always real in space and time. Creative action is the experience of what is alive, as experienced from the inside, subjectively. One might say it is based on "affective objectivity"—a universal and real phenomenon, but one that is also evanescent and resistant to measurement.

Indian geographer Neera Singh has shown the extent to which this emotive power encourages commoners to act and provides subjective rewards for their action. She demonstrates that villagers in rural India not only make resources more productive through their commoning with forests; they also satisfy emotional needs and "transform their individual and collective subjectivities."[13] They are engaging in an active poetics of relating, in which the human affect and the material world commune with each other and alter one another.

It bears emphasizing that the "collective subjectivity" extends beyond the human community to include the subjectivities of the living environment—the trees, the supportive vegetation, the birds, the flows of water, the "real" ecosystem elements that human subjectivities actually transform. Commoners, one could say, follow a *poetic reason* that has emotive substance, but also material manifestations in people's bodies, community life, and local ecosystems. The poetic moment of their action manifests itself when the living forest and social community flourish together, in entangled synergy—something that can be perceived by the senses and can be experienced emotionally through the forest's opulent biodiversity (and yes, can also be measured, but the measurements will invariably fail to grasp the animating power of the human affect).

It is telling that cultures for which participation in natural processes amounts to emotional engagement in a poetic reality make no distinctions between "animate" and "inanimate" or "nature" and "culture"—dualities that are taken for granted in Western thinking. The basic affective experience of being in a lively exchange with the world, taking from it and contributing to it, is denied by the Western worldview and language: a perniciously subliminal type of enclosure.

Singh calls the psychological-emotional engagement arising from caring for a commons "emotional work." In the absence of this affective dimension, both subject and object lose their paired identities: those working on the land, say, as well as the object of such work, the animate whole. Geographers and philosophers are increasingly beginning to comprehend land and people as a lived reality—a factor of real interactions and an existential, poetic enactment.

If such a commons is colonialized—which today would mean being reduced to a mere resource by industrial agriculture—the emotional needs (belonging, meaning, identity) of the people involved can no longer be fulfilled. This is precisely what has happened to our purportedly modern minds—a colonization of emotions that are denounced as backward, superstitious, unenlightened, or unscientific. The emotional work of caring for a commons, however, is both an ecological necessity and a material reality, as well as a psychological need. Therefore the collapse of affect (belonging, meaning, identity) has material consequences. As human relationships to an ecosystem erode, so does respect for the ecosystem, as well as the ecosystem's stability. A kind of ecological death then occurs that has both spiritual and biodiversity-related dimensions. The two depend on and balance one another.

In other words, a healthy culture is a co-creative interpretation of nature in all its irrepressible aliveness. That is why subjectivity, cooperation, negotiation, and irreconcilable otherness must not be seen as patterns that only we place upon the world, as most economic and cultural frameworks tend to posit as a given. It is in fact the other way around: subjectivity, meaning-creation, "weak" noncausal interaction, code, and interpretation are deep features of living nature. Its most basic principle comes down to an individual's paradoxical self-realization, which is only possible through interacting with the whole, whereby the whole at the same time needs to be to be fenced off as other. Need, distance, and momentary balance in beauty: Aliveness as such is a commoning process. Perception thus becomes a co-creative commons integrating a subject concerned with care for its self and its environment—which both mutually imagine, nourish, and bring forth one another. From this perspective, our deeper feelings are themselves a distinguishing feature of patterns of creative aliveness. They affect subjective perception and compel us to participate in a co-creative commons with our environment; subjects and environment actively imagine, nourish, and engender each other.

Culture is not structurally different from nature. It is not the "human sphere" in opposition to something entirely other—a feature setting humankind apart as incommensurate with the remainder of the world. Nor does nature underlie human culture in any reductionist sense: cultural structures cannot be explained through sociobiological means. The causal-mechanic, efficiency-centered approach as a whole is mistaken. Nature is basically meaning-centered, open to creative change, bringing forth agents with subjective experiences and always creative in realizing the individual through the whole. It generates feelings to accompany any exchange-relationship, which is always both metabolism and meaning. Nature is a process of unfolding freedom, tapping into inexhaustible creativity, and intensifying experiential and expressive depth.

It is in this sense, and not via any superficial reductionistic pattern, that culture must be like nature. This is an idea somewhat parallel to what philosopher Theodor W. Adorno claimed when he argued that art worthy of its name does not copy nature's objects but rather follows its deep process of creative unfolding, freedom, and "non-identity."[14]

Culture echoes ecological exchange processes in the human species-specific creative form. It expresses our own poetic interpretation of the ever-reoccurring theme of coping with the irresolvable paradox of autonomy and wholeness. That is why human culture cannot control and engineer nature as a passive, nonliving object. Since we humans are implicated in the creative aliveness of nature, our culture must also honor our own aliveness as the best way to foster our own freedom and long-term survival: as shaping our paradoxical autonomy-in-relation according to the needs of a larger whole that is necessary to all life.

CULTURE AS BRAVERY OF BEING

Getting to know ourselves is the task of a culture of life. A culture of life strives for insight into the creative principles of aliveness in order to imagine them anew for ourselves. To make this possible we need something we could call a "bravery of being." We need to face the limits of reality, the shortcomings of our own existence, our own death, in order to do what is necessary. We must be as determined to serve aliveness as a water ouzel searching for food in a mountain stream in the dead of winter: because we cannot be otherwise.

Bravery of being requires that we unlearn brainhood. It means that we must confront the fact that we are alive and therefore mortal, that we have needs that express themselves with poetic insistence. These needs cannot be controlled, only repressed, because they are the truth of the flesh that unconsciously wants itself. A new culture must seek this truth and speak it out aloud. In order to make this possible, it imagines our naturalness in the medium of humankind. It imagines the other through ourselves, and ourselves through the other. From this perspective, culture is no longer that which sets us fundamentally apart from the other. It centers on the other in order to allow the self to unfold. Its goal is to make us into what we already are: selfhood-in-connection.

To take culture for something that differentiates us humans from other beings is a fundamental error. If we buy into the cultural belief of human particularity, we may (according to temperament and preference) celebrate or deplore the fact that this particularity determines the fate of the planet and convert it into a well-kept garden or the bleak suburbia of Mad Max (or even, depending on income and neighborhood, both). Culture is for many, who today welcome the end of dualism and revel in the reconciliation of humanity and creation, still a specifically human affair.

But a culture that does not take part in the inner makeup of aliveness and its principles, which are a magnification of the principles of reality, will by necessity destroy this aliveness. For it is aliveness that spreads the fundamental tension which culture needs to mediate. Culture can only decide to carry out this mediation in a more or less toxic way. At the moment, in this world that identifies the living as the problem and from this attribution presumes to develop "solutions" for a "better life," we are all in great need of therapy.

We can use the Anthropocene as an opportunity to seriously consider the fact that humans are entangled with other beings and biochemical cycles. We will succeed in reshaping the picture of ourselves if we imagine this entanglement with the cosmos through a poetics of embodied relatedness. Only then will we experience in our bodies the fact that the fertile powers of reality cannot be separated into the dual spheres of human versus nature. The rules of aliveness can be obeyed only if we remain totally entangled. This means accepting that we today are the Earth's de facto gardeners, turning the landscape over and leveling the surface of the planet. But we must also see that telluric forces, self-organization, and the shape-changing desire of complex systems to experience themselves as being alive are elements of ourselves, which cannot be kept in check and under control, but must be embodied by our own aliveness.

Culture must imagine the desire of the living in such a way that does not destroy the biosphere but enhances it. Culture does not have to realize more than the continuation of the principle that there be life. It has to do this in the imaginative sphere of the human, not in that of anchoas or monarch butterflies. These creatures enact their aliveness without thinking about it, as sensual, wistful eddies in a cascade of metamorphoses. We, however, must make an explicit decision as to how we want to partake in these transformations.

We need culture because we are the only beings who cannot experience ecological integration before we've already imagined and structured it. Where anchoas and monarch butterflies simply enact their niche, we must invent it by understanding what is required for us to enact our individuality through the fertility of the whole. This requirement must not be followed blindly. Imagination is necessary in order to follow what is necessary. It does not decouple us from necessity, it allows us to dance with it. That we as humans need to invent our place in ecology does not raise us over the principles of aliveness, but must instead make them more salient in our existence. Human culture must use imagination to reinvent what is already there, just as poets do. That is what makes us the poetic species. But it does not free us from the necessities that come with being a part of the larger context of fertile reciprocity. Because we are the poetic species, we must design our connection to the other; we must conceive it and make it effective as a cultural process. This means being continuously active in a life-giving way. The task of culture is to enact the conditions of naturalness through unique imagination. And culture, too, can only produce freedom from the insight into necessity, just as the water ouzel does on a cold mountain morning.

This attitude is not deterministic; the naturalness I am talking about does not determine us, but rather involves us in a process of freedom. The center of this reality is a process of fertile unfolding. This fertile unfolding is the living process itself. The experience of aliveness is the revelation of this fertility, experienced from the inside, as its subject in structure and in feeling. Our culture can be nothing but the creative interpretation of nature and of the commons of mutual transformation, from which it rises and which cannot ever be suppressed.

Individuals and the biosphere encompass both material processes and relations of meaning. Together they constitute lived experience, which from within is subjectively "felt" and from without exhibits itself as that which is "sensuous" and "expressive." This poetic space is not to be confused with the juxtaposition of "spirit" (inside) and "body" (outside). The polarity of poetic space shows both as conjoined, metamorphic material that is always meaningful. This idea breaks with any notion of primacy of either matter or symbolic relationships, and so in this way is radically nondualistic.

There is no outside to poetic space because poetic space encompasses both organic and nonorganic matter. Culture has to shape this poetic space. At the same time, the imaginary material of this poetic space can be subject to transformation from both "sides": through material manipulation, but also through imaginative creation. Poetic space is open to new interpretations, new utterances of self-expression, and can be transformed in such a way that real change in the world will take place. It follows from these ideas that culture as a process of imagining and transforming reality has its greatest potential to be alive if it is a poetic—or artistic—process.

We can quickly escape the habit of thinking in terms of culture versus nature if we accept that everything is in continuous exchange—as the body that exchanges all its atoms with the environment every few years through the process of metabolism. Through these changes, the amount of different experiences—felt depth—grows over time. Life is about making more and more experiences. It itself is enlivening. The fact is that we do have an inborn instinct for seeking out new experiences that reveal how it is to be inside life. We follow a drive to do the same as the world does: deepen our experiences, extend our knowledge of ourselves and others, unfold new capacities, strengthen bonds, and so on. One might say that this process is about learning to respect and learning to love.

Culture is the interpretation of our aliveness through the medium of human beings. It implies the creative imagination of what is real. Subjectivity, cooperation, negotiation, and incompatible strangeness are not patterns that we place on the world. These patterns are themselves nature. They authenticate perception as a co-creative commons of self-creating subjects and surroundings in which both mutually transform one another.

In this respect, culture—the intermediate, the vicarious, the creative exchange—is our nature. This nature is not opposed to nature "out there," but is one of its appearances.

Therefore culture cannot control and engineer nature. It cannot free itself from the principles of fertile imagination without destroying it. But it can very well become a culture of our aliveness, which in creative freedom jointly spawns what is necessary for ongoing mutual transformation. Humanity is the manner in which the Earth imagines itself when it is allowed to dream the unlimited. When human beings dream the unlimited, they are required to imagine it as Earth. Only that is a culture of true reciprocity.

CULTURE AS FINDING OURSELVES IN OTHERS

The paradox of culture is this: to become fully human, we need the relationship to that which is emphatically nonhuman—we need the interbeing with living selves that are alien to ourselves. We have to become animal in order to be human. The consoling fact is that we are already animal. We only need to let ourselves believe it.

In the republic of innumerable species and existential relational processes, all contradictions can be embedded without being flattened out. This is one of the core experiences in the presence of other beings. Through the deep emotions that natural settings are able to provoke in their human participants, complementarities can exist in balance: that life is a gift and a burden; that necessity must be obeyed in order to set you free; that death is painful, but a requirement for birth. All this is written down nowhere, but continuously enacted through the unknowing wisdom of commoning among myriad feeling bodies, plants, and organisms.

Plants and animals are not just abstract models for relations. They are relations in their very enactment. At the same time, living beings are the embodied mediation of the paradoxes underlying life. They are closed unto themselves, as any living being is, yet they are also open and vulnerable. Something rests in the middle of their being that is accessible and yet absolutely unfathomable. It is not alien, but it is without limits. They are what Goethe referred to as *Urphänomen*—"primordial phenomenon." This is something that is inscrutable but also its own explication—though only as a phenomenon, not as an explanation or an algorithm.

Nature and its principle of contradictions that yield meaningful experiences is also "inside" ourselves. It is not too far-fetched to claim that in order to experience a fertile identity, we are dependent on the presence of forests, rivers, oceans, meadows, deserts, and wild animals. In some respect, only the other—another living presence—can give life to the self. We gather food for our thoughts and mental concepts from the natural world. We transform plants and animals into intellectual symbols according to their real or presumed qualities. The snake, the rose, and the tree are each examples of powerful organic images that speak to our human identity, which is why they recur so often throughout human history in our art, myths, and other cultural forms.

This process also works in reverse. Nature embodies what we are, too. It is the living—and enlivening—counterpart of our emotions and our mental concepts. Only by being perceived and reflected by other lives can we understand our own. Only in the eyes of another being can we ourselves become a living being. We need the regard of the most unknown in order to come to terms with that which is part of us but beyond our grasp. We need to be touched by matter in order to understand that we are matter. This reciprocal way of building up our identity is one of the most prominent cultural constants, from the use of animal symbols of indigenous peoples such as the Aboriginal Australians (e.g., in rock art) to the constant application of nature metaphors in contemporary poetry.

Obviously, such a practice can release those layers of feeling in ourselves that otherwise remain locked up. We need the experience of engaging with a "living inside" that stands in front of us, displaying itself as a fragile, mortal body. We need other organisms because they are in a very real sense what we ourselves are (biologically and psychically), and they give us access to those hidden parts of ourselves that we cannot see. We cannot observe ourselves. There is always a blind spot central to the establishment of our own identity. Other beings constitute this blind spot of our self-understanding. We must be given the chance to grasp the whole world in the other, and the other in ourselves. We need to meet our own eyes in their gaze, while we desire to be ourselves, as all beings do, by being fully of this shared world.

In the presence of wild nature, be it as taxonomically close to us as an ape or as seemingly infinitely distant as a tadpole, we find ourselves among speechless yet eloquent creation. The animal's gaze upon us is woven from the entanglement of the most intimately known with the most alien. It is the most enlivening gaze imaginable. The distinctness of many of our experiential categories is possible only because in wild nature, in *natura naturans*, there is this form of embodied and hence objectified subjectivity, which shares our own.

Could it be that this embodied subjectivity has brought us forth and still dwells within us, guiding our responses as to how to confront our own embodied existence? Here seems to lie a path along which dualism can be healed. The deep cleft that has opened up between us and other beings, between the world as we experience it and the world as we describe it, closes and reintegrates. For the first time in a long period, in this space, we are welcome. The deep cleft closes not to beckon us toward a utopian dream, but to allow us to experience a moment of awareness.

Plato had suggested that for every term, be it as abstract as can be, there is an *eidos*, an archetype in the empire of ideas. Plato was certainly mistaken on this point. The empire of ideas does not lie beyond, in an ideal world, but is anchored here, in the bodies of plants and animals, in the buzz of the bees and in the shape described by the circling raven.

Notes

INTRODUCTION

1. Gary Snyder, quoted in Tom Butler, "Lives not Our Own," in *Keeping the Wild: Against the Domestication of the Earth*, ed. George Wuerthner, Eileen Crist, and Tom Butler (Washington, DC: Island Press, 2014), viii.

2. Andreas Weber, "Reality as Commons," in *Patterns of Commoning*, ed. David Bollier and Silke Helfrich (Amherst, MA: Levellers Press, 2015).

3. For an introduction, see David Bollier, *Think Like a Commoner: A Short Introduction to the Life of the Commons* (Gladiola Island, BC: New Society, 2014), and David Bollier and Silke Helfrich, *Free, Fair and Alive* (Gabriola Island, BC: New Society Press, 2019).

4. Stephan Harding, *Animate Earth: Science, Intuition and Gaia*, 2nd ed. (Dartington, UK: Green Books, 2009); Bruno Latour, *Facing Gaia: Eight Lectures on the New Climatic Regime* (New York: Wiley, 2017).

5. Simone Weil, *La Pesanteur et la* Grâce (Paris: Plon, 1988).

6. For an extended argument, see Andreas Weber, *Matter and Desire: An Erotic Ecology* (White River Junction: Chelsea Green, 2017).

7. See, e.g., Timothy Morton, *Humankind: Solidarity with Nonhuman People* (New York: Verso, 2017).

8. See Édouard Glissant, *Philosophie de la relation: Poésie en étendue* (Paris: Gallimard, 2009).

9. My heartfelt gratitude to Heike Löschmann of Heinrich-Böll-Foundation, Berlin, who in her usual deft manner in

addressing the most serious things coined this term in an informal talk in the presence of the author, on November 15, 2012.

10. Amir Engel, *Gershom Scholem. An Intellectual Biography* (Chicago: University of Chicago Press, 2017), 75ff.

CHAPTER 1

1. Elizabeth Kolbert, *The Sixth Extinction: An Unnatural History* (New York: Macmillan, 2015).

2. Gro Harlem Brundlandt, *Our Common Future: Report of the World Commission on Environment and Development* (United Nations, 1987).

3. Nancy MacLean, *Democracy in Chains: The Deep History of the Radical Right's Stealth Plan for America* (New York: Penguin Random House, 2017).

4. Richard Layard, *Happiness: Lessons from a New Science* (London: Penguin, 2005), 29. See also Robert E. Lane, *The Loss of Happiness in Market Democracies* (New Haven, CT: Yale University Press), 20.

5. Deborah Wan, "Foreword," in *Depression: A Global Crisis* (World Federation for Mental Health, 2012), 2.

6. Occam's razor is a scientific principle of parsimony stating that, among competing explanations, the one that makes the simplest and fewest assumptions is the correct one.

7. See Max Horkheimer and Theodor W. Adorno, *Dialectic of Enlightenment* (New York: Continuum, 1969).

8. Francesca Ferrando, "Posthumanism, Transhumanism, Antihumanism, Metahumanism, and New Materialisms: Differences and Relations," *Existenz* 8, no. 2 (2013): 26–32.

9. Theodor W. Adorno, *Negative Dialectics* (London: A&C Black, 1973), 406.

10. This term was coined by David Abram, *The Spell of the Sensuous: Perception and Language in a More Than Human World* (New York: Pantheon, 1996).

11. For an in-depth exploration from a biopoetical point of view, see Andreas Weber, "Cognition as Expression: On the Autopoietic Foundations of an Aesthetic Theory of Nature," *Sign System Studies* 29, no. 1 (2001): 153–168; Weber, "The Book of Desire: Towards a Biological Poetics," *Biosemiotics* 4, no. 2 (2010): 32–58; Weber, "There Is No Outside: A Biological Corollary for Poetic Space," in *Gatherings in Biosemiotics: Tartu Semiotics Library 11*, ed. Silver Rattasepp and Tyler Bennett (Tartu: University of Tartu Press, 2012), 225–226; Weber, *The Biology of Wonder: Aliveness, Meaning and the Metamorphosis of Science* (Gabriola Island, BC: New Society, 2016); Weber, *Matter and Desire: An Erotic Ecology* (White River Junction: Chelsea Green, 2017).

12. Storm Cunningham, *reWealth! Stake Your Claim in the $2 Trillion reDevelopment Trend That's Renewing the World* (Washington: McGraw Hill, 2008).

13. Herman E. Daly and Joshua Farley, *Ecological Economics: Principles and Applications* (Washington, DC: Island Press, 2004).

14. Ralf Fücks, *Intelligent wachsen: Die grüne Revolution* (Munich: Hanser, 2013); Thomas L. Friedman, *Hot, Flat and Crowded: Why the World Needs a Green Revolution and How We Can Renew Our Global Future* (New York: Farrar, Strauss and Giroux, 2008). See also Andreas Weber, *Biokapital: Die Versöhnung von Ökonomie, Natur und Menschlichkeit* (Berlin: Berlin-Verlag, 2008).

15. Lynn Margulis, *Symbiotic Planet: A New Look at Evolution* (New York: Basic Books, 1999); Francisco J. Varela, Evan T. Thompson, and Eleanor Rosch, *The Embodied Mind: Cognitive Science and Human Experience* (Cambridge, MA: MIT Press, 1993); Terrence Deacon, *Incomplete Nature: How Mind Emerged from Matter* (Boston: Norton, 2012); Stuart Kauffman, *At Home in the Universe: The Search for the Laws of Self-Organization and Complexity* (Washington, DC: American Chemical Society, 1996); Antonio Damasio, *The Feeling of What Happens: Body and Emotion in the Making*

of Consciousness (New York: Harcourt Brace, 2000); David Abram, *The Spell of the Sensuous: Perception and Language in a More-Than-Human-World* (New York: Pantheon, 1997).

16. For an extended analysis of the current "quantum leap" in biology, see Andreas Weber, *Biopoetics: Towards an Existential Ecology* (Dordrecht: Springer, 2016), esp. chap. 13, "Conatus."

17. Edward O. Wilson, *The Social Conquest of Earth* (New York: Norton, 2013).

18. For a profound analysis of the gift as provider of cosmic fertility, see Lewis Hyde, *The Gift: Imagination and the Erotic Life of Property* (New York: Random House, 1983).

19. Hildegard Kurt, *Wachsen! Über das Geistige in der Nachhaltigkeit* (Stuttgart: Johannes M. Mayer, 2010); Shelley Sacks and Hildegard Kurt, *Die rote Blume: Ästhetische Praxis in Zeiten des Wandels*, with a foreword by Wolfgang Sachs (Klein Jasedow: thinkOya, 2013).

20. Maurice Merleau-Ponty, *Le visible et l'invisible* (Paris: Gallimard, 1964).

21. See http://en.wikipedia.org/wiki/Fundamental_human_needs; Manfred A. Max-Neef, *Human Scale Development: Conception, Application and Further Reflections* (New York: Apex Press, 1991).

CHAPTER 2

1. Hans Blumenberg, *Paradigms for a Metaphorology* (Ithaca, NY: Cornell University Press, 2016; original German publication 1960).

2. Andreas Weber, "Natural Anticapitalism," in *The Wealth of the Commons: A World beyond Market and State*, ed. David Bollier and Silke Helfrich (Amherst, MA: Levellers Press, 2012), http://wealthofthecommons.org/.

3. See Barrington Moore Jr., *Social Origins of Dictatorship and Democracy: Lord and Peasant in the Making of the Modern World* (Boston: Beacon Press, 1966).

4. Léon Walras, *Elements of Pure Economics* (London: Routledge, 1954); W. Stanley Jevons, *The Theory of Political Economy* (London: MacMillan, 1871). For discussion, see Andreas Weber, *Biokapital: Die Versöhnung von Ökonomie, Natur und Menschlichkeit* (Berlin: Berlin-Verlag, 2008).

5. For a discussion on our limited ability to identify relationships in any given system, see Donella Meadows, *Thinking in Systems: A Primer*, ed. Diana Wright, Sustainability Institute (White River Junction: Chelsea Green, 2008).

6. Karl Polanyi, *The Great Transformation: Political and Economic Origins of Our Time* (Boston: Beacon Press, 1944); Polanyi, *The Livelihood of Man: Studies in Social Discontinuity*, ed. Harry Pearson (New York: Academic Press, 1977).

7. Paul Shephard, *Coming Home to the Pleistocene* (Washington, DC: Island Press, 1998).

8. John Maynard Keynes, "The Future," in *Essays in Persuasion* (London: W. W. Norton, 1991).

9. Parts of this section were previously published in Weber, "Reality as Commons," in *Patterns of Commoning*, ed. David Bollier and Silke Helfrich (Amherst, MA: Levellers Press, 2015).

10. David Johns, "With Friends Like These, Wilderness and Biodiversity Do Not Need Enemies," in *Keeping the Wild: Against the Domestication of the Earth*, ed. George Wuerthner, Eileen Crist, Tom Butler (Washington, DC: Island Press, 2014), 42.

11. Manfred Max-Neef, "Development and Human Needs," in *Real-Life Economics*, ed. Paul Ekins and Manfred Max-Neef (London: Routledge, 1992).

12. David W. Kidner, "The Conceptual Assassination of Wilderness," in *Keeping the Wild*, 10.

13. Bruno Latour, "Love Your Monsters: Why We Must Care for Our Technologies as We Do Our Children," in *Love Your Monsters: Postenvironmentalism and the Anthropocene*, ed. Michael Schellenberger and Ted Nordhaus (Oakland: The Breakthrough Institute, 2011).

14 See David Bollier, *Think Like a Commoner: A Short Introduction to the Life of the Commons* (Gladiola Island, BC: New Society, 2014).

15. Stuart Kauffman, *At Home in the Universe: The Search for Laws of Self-Organization and Complexity* (Oxford: Oxford University Press, 1995).

16. For a brilliant demonstration of this regarding the example of the fauna of Madagascar, see Miguel Vences et al., "Madagascar as a Model Region of Species Diversification," *Trends in Ecology and Evolution* 24, no. 8 (2009): 456–465.

CHAPTER 3

1. For a book-length elaboration of the position presented in this chapter, see Andreas Weber, *Biopoetics: Toward an Existential Ecology* (Dordrecht: Springer, 2016).

2. Richard Strohmann, "The Coming Kuhnian Revolution in Biology," *Nature Biotechnology* 15 (1997): 194–199.

3. Eva Jablonka and Marion Lamb, *Evolution in Four Dimensions: Genetic, Epigenetic, Behavioral, and Symbolic Variation in the History of Life* (Cambridge, MA: MIT Press, 2005).

4. Joachim Bauer, *Das kooperative Gen* (Hamburg: Hoffmann und Campe, 2008).

5. Don Powell, "Treat a Female Rat Like a Male and Its Brain Changes," *New Scientist* 2690 (2009): 8.

6. Ruth E. Ley, Catherine A. Lozupone, Micah Hamady, Rob Knight, and Jeffrey I. Gordon, "Worlds within Worlds: Evolution of the Vertebrate Gut Microbiota," *Nature Reviews* 6 (2008): 776–788.

7. Humberto R. Maturana and Francisco J. Varela, *Autopoiesis and Cognition: The Realization of the Living* (Boston: D. Reidel, 1980).

8. Marc W. Kirschner and John C. Gerhart, *The Plausibility of Life: Resolving Darwin's Dilemma* (New Haven, CT: Yale University Press, 2005).

9. For a detailed overview, see Andreas Weber and Francisco Varela, "Life after Kant: Natural Purposes and the Autopoietic Foundations of Biological Individuality," *Phenomenology and the Cognitive Sciences* 1 (2002): 97–125; Andreas Weber, "The Book of Desire: Towards a Biological Poetics," *Biosemiotics* 4, no. 2 (2010): 32–58.

10. Francisco J. Varela, "Patterns of Life: Intertwining Identity and Cognition," *Brain and Cognition* 34 (1997): 72–87.

11. For the incompatibility argument, see Kalevi Kull, "Introduction," in *Gatherings in Biosemiotics: Tartu Semiotics Library 11*, ed. Silver Rattasepp and Tyler Bennett (Tartu: University of Tartu Press, 2012).

12. Francisco J. Varela, "Organism: A Meshwork of Selfless Selves," in *Organism and the Origins of Self*, ed. I. Tauber (Dordrecht: Kluwer, 1991).

13. Weber, *The Biology of Wonder: Aliveness, Meaning and the Metamorphosis of Science* (Gabriola Island, BC: New Society, 2016).

14. Gregory Bateson and Mary Catherine Bateson, *Angels Fear: Towards An Epistemology of the Sacred* (New York: Hampton Press, 2004).

15. Bateson and Bateson, *Angels Fear*.

CHAPTER 4

1. See Elinor Ostrom, *Future of the Commons: Beyond Market Failure and Government Regulations* (London: Institute of Economic Affairs, 2012); David Bollier and Silke Helfrich, eds., *The Wealth of the Commons: A World beyond Market*

and State (Amherst, MA: Levellers Press, 2012), http://wealthofthecommons.org/.

2. For the term "Stone Age economics," see Marshall D. Sahlins, *Stone Age Economics* (New York: De Gruyter, 1972). Sahlins calculated that an individual's daily working hours in Stone Age societies did not exceed six hours, with which food and shelter could be obtained in a sufficient manner. Therefore the anthropologist called this model of civilization the "original affluent society." See also Andreas Weber, *Indigenialität* (Berlin: Nicolai, 2018).

3. For a detailed argument, see Philippe Descola, *Par-delà nature et culture* (Paris: Gallimard, 2005).

4. Timothy Garton Ash, "It Always Lies Below: A Hurricane Produces Anarchy. Decivilization Is Not as Far Away as We Like to Think," *Guardian*, September 2005, 8.

5. Rebecca Solnit, *A Paradise Built in Hell: The Extraordinary Communities That Arise in Disaster* (London: Penguin, 2010).

6. John Rawls, *A Theory of Justice* (Cambridge, MA: Harvard University Press, 1971).

7. John Muir, *My First Summer in the Sierra* (Boston: Houghton Mifflin Harcourt, 2011).

8. Francisco J. Varela, Evan Thompson, and Eleanor Rosch, *The Embodied Mind: Cognitive Science and Human Experience* (Cambridge, MA: MIT Press, 1991).

9. Humberto R. Maturana and Francisco J. Varela, *Autopoiesis and Cognition: The Realization of the Living* (Boston: D. Reidel, 1980).

10. Francisco J. Varela, "Patterns of Life: Intertwining Identity and Cognition," *Brain and Cognition* 34 (1997): 72–87.

11. Terrence Deacon, *The Symbolic Species: The Co-Evolution of Language and the Brain* (New York: W. W. Norton, 1997).

12. Miguel Benasayag and Gérard Schmit, *L'epoca delle passioni tristi* (Milan: Feltrinelli, 2007).

13. Gerald Manley Hopkins, "Pied Beauty," in *The Classic Hundred Poems*, ed. William Harmon (New York: Columbia University Press, 1998).

CHAPTER 5

1. Jonathan Rowe, *Our Common Wealth: The Hidden Economy That Makes Everything Else Work* (San Francisco: Berrett-Koehler, 2013).

2. Ruth Meinzen-Dick et al., *Securing the Commons 1* (CAPRi Policy Brief No. 4, May 2006), http:/www.capri.cgiar.org/pdf/polbrief_04.pdf.

3. David Bollier, *Think Like a Commoner: A Short Introduction to the Life of the Commons* (Gladiola Island, BC: New Society, 2014), 174.

4. In addition, "fair use" industries that rely on the copying and sharing of copyrighted work—educational institutions, manufacturers of consumer devices that enable copying, Internet search and Internet service providers, and others—account for one-sixth of the US gross domestic product. Michael Bauwens et al., *Synthetic Overview of the Collaborative Economy*, P2P Foundation (2012).

5. Arun Agarwal, "Common Resources and Institutional Sustainability," in *The Drama of the Commons* (National Research Council, Committee on the Human Dimensions of Global Change, 2002), 42.

6. Michael Safi, "Suicides of Nearly 60,000 Indian Farmers Linked to Climate Change, Study Claims," *Guardian*, July 31, 2017.

7. Gustavo Soto Santiesteban and Silke Helfrich, "*El Buen Vivir* and the Commons," in *The Wealth of the Commons: A World beyond Market and State*, ed. David Bollier and Silke Helfrich (Amherst, MA: Levellers Press, 2012), 278, http://wealthof thecommons.org/.

8. Andreas Weber and Reiner Klingholz, *Demografischer Wandel: Ein Politikvorschlag unter besonderer Berücksichtigung der Neuen Länder* (Berlin: Berlin-Institut für Demografie und Entwicklung, 2009).

9. See, e.g., Joseph E. Stiglitz, "Markets, Market Failures, and Development," *American Economic Review* 79, no. 2 (1989): 197–203.

10. Donella Meadows, *Thinking in Systems: A Primer*, ed. Diana Wright, Sustainability Institute (White River Junction: Chelsea Green, 2008).

11. Wendell Berry, *Life Is a Miracle: An Essay against Modern Superstition* (Boston: Counterpoint Press, 2000).

12. Charles Schweik, a leading American social scientist and commons scholar who has studied why some open source software projects succeed and others fail, finds that multidimensional engagement is the best predictor of successful projects—an idea that he calls "a theory of compound incentives." Charles Schweik, *Internet Success: A Study of Open-Source Software Commons* (Cambridge, MA: MIT Press, 2012).

13. Manfred Max-Neef, "Development and Human Needs," in *Real-Life Economics*, ed. Paul Ekins and Manfred Max-Neef (London: Routledge, 1992), 206–207.

14. For Max-Neef's matrix of human needs, see Philip B. Smith and Manfred Max-Neef, *Economics Unmasked: From Power and Greed to Compassion and the Common Good* (Totnes: Green Books, 2012), 143.

15. For an important synopsis in German, see Christa Müller, ed., *Urban Gardening: Über die Rückkehr der Gärten in die Stadt* (Munich: Oekom, 2011).

16. Gregory Bateson and Mary Catherine Bateson, *Angels Fear: Towards An Epistemology of the Sacred* (New York: Hampton Press, 2004).

17. David Bollier, "The Commons," http://www.publicsphereproject.org/node/201.

18. See Christopher Alexander, *The Nature of Order: An Essay on the Art of Building and the Nature of the Universe, Book 1—The Phenomenon of Life* (Oxford: Routledge, 2004). See also Helmut Leitner, *Pattern Theory: Introduction and Perspectives on the Tracks of Christopher Alexander* (CreateSpace Independent Publishing Platform, 2015); Shierry Weber Nicholsen (2004): "Art-Making as a Process of Creating Aliveness: A Review of Christopher Alexander's *The Nature of Order: An Essay on the Art of Building and the Nature of the Universe*," http://home.earthlink.net/~snicholsen/sitebuildercontent/sitebuilderfiles/creating-aliveness-on-christopher-alexander.doc. For the existential and meaningful aesthetics argument, see also Andreas Weber, "Cognition as Expression: On the Autopoietic Foundations of an Aesthetic Theory of Nature," *Sign System Studies* 29, no. 1 (2001): 153–168.

19. Quoted by Franz Nahrada, "The Commoning of Patterns and the Patterns of Commoning," in *The Wealth of the Commons*.

20. For a detailed development of applied principles how this form of commons householding could be designed, see Burns H. Weston and David Bollier, *Green Governance: Ecological Survival, Human Rights, and the Law of the Commons* (Cambridge: Cambridge University Press, 2013). For further discussion on the principles of biospheric householding, see also Weber, *Biokapital: Die Versöhnung von Ökonomie, Natur und Menschlichkeit* (Berlin: Berlin-Verlag, 2008), chaps. 5–7.

21. See, e.g., Bollier and Helfrich, *The Wealth of the Commons*.

22. For an extended discussion on the meaning of play, see Andreas Weber, *Mehr Matsch: Kinder brauchen Natur* (Berlin: Ullstein-Verlag, 2011). For a profound introduction to "original play" as deep understanding of reality, see also O. Fred Donaldson, *Playing by Heart: The Vision and Practice of*

Belonging (Deerfield Beach, FL: Health Communications, 1993).

23. Quoted by Nahrada, "The Commoning of Patterns."

CHAPTER 6

1. Marshall B. Rosenberg, *Nonviolent Communication: A Language of Life: Create Your Life, Your Relationships, and Your World in Harmony with Your Values* (Encinitas, CA: Puddle Dancer Press, 2003).

2. Andreas Weber, *Sein und Teilen: Eine Praxis schöpferischer Existenz* (Bielefeld: transcript, 2017).

3. Consider J. M. Coetzee's critique of Thomas Nagel's essay "What Is It Like to Be a Bat?": "To be a living bat is to be full of being. Bat-being in the first case, human-being in the second, maybe; but those are secondary considerations. To be full of being is to live as a body-soul. One name for the experience of full being is *joy.*" J. M. Coetzee, *The Lives of Animals* (Princeton, NJ: Princeton University Press, 1999), 33.

4. I. G. Campbell-Fisher, "Aesthetics and the Logic of Sense," *Journal of General Psychology* 43 (1950): 245–273.

5. Aldo Leopold, *A Sand County Almanac* (Madison: University of Wisconsin Press, 1944).

6. Leopold, "Marshland Elegy," in *A Sand County Almanac*, 129.

7. See Gary Snyder, *No Nature: New and Selected Poems* (New York: Pantheon, 1992).

8. Some interesting attempts to generalize a first-person ecology in a more systematic way include work by the French physicist and philosopher Michel Bitbol. Michel Bitbol, "Panpsychism in the First Person," in *Analytic and Continental Philosophy: Methods and Perspectives: Proceedings of the 37th International Wittgenstein Symposium*, ed. Harald A. Wiltsche and Sonja Rinofner-Kreidl (Berlin: De Gruyter, 2016), 79–94.

9. Sacha Kagan, *Toward Global Environmental Change: Transformative Art and Cultures of Sustainability* (Berlin: Heinrich-Böll-Stiftung, 2011), http://www.boell.de.

10. Amen Avanessian, *Überschrift: Ethik des Wissens—Poetik der Existenz* (Berlin: Merve, 2015).

11. Bruno Latour, *We Have Never Been Modern* (Cambridge, MA: Harvard University Press, 1993).

12. Henry Miller, "Reflections on Writing," in *Wisdom of the Heart* (New York: New Directions, 1960).

13. Francisco J. Varela et al., eds., *Naturalizing Phenomenology: Issues in Contemporary Phenomenology and Cognitive Science* (Stanford: Stanford University Press, 1999).

14. Francisco J. Varela, Evan Thompson, and Eleanor Rosch, *The Embodied Mind: Cognitive Science and Human Experience* (Cambridge, MA: MIT Press, 1991); Andreas Weber, "Die wiedergefundene Welt," in *Schlüsselwerke des Konstruktivismus*, ed. Bernhard Pörksen (Bielefeld: VS-Verlag, 2011).

15. Francisco J. Varela, "Organism: A Meshwork of Selfless Selves," in *Organism and the Origins of Self*, ed. A. I. Tauber (Dordrecht: Kluwer, 1991).

16. Jon Young, Ellen Haas, and Evan McGown, *Coyote's Guide to Connecting with Nature* (Shelton: OWLink Media, 2008).

17. Franz Rosenzweig, "Das älteste Systemprogramm des deutschen Idealismus: Ein handschriftlicher Fund," in *Sitzungsberichte der Heidelberger Akademie der Wissenschaften* (Heidelberg: Universitätsverlag C. Winter, 1917).

18. Elizabeth Sewell, *The Orphic Voice: Poetry and Natural History* (Washington, DC: Routledge, 1961).

19. Friedrich Hölderlin, "The Oldest System-Program of German Idealism," in *Friedrich Hölderlin: Essays and Letters on Theory*, ed. Thomas Pfau (Albany: SUNY Press, 1987), 155.

20. Quoted by Joan Rothfuss, Walker Art Center curator, "Energy," http://www.walkerart.org.

21. Daniel C. Wahl, "'Zarte Empirie': Goethean Science as a Way of Knowing," *Janus Head* 8, no. 1 (2005): 58–76.

22. Andreas Weber and Hildegard Kurt, "Towards Cultures of Aliveness: Politics and Poetics in a Postdualistic Age—An Anthropocene Manifesto," *Solutions Journal* 5 (2015).

CHAPTER 7

1. Edouard Glissant, "Comme l'oiseau innumerable," in *La cohée du Lamentin: Poétique V* (Paris: Gallimard, 2005).

2. Edouard Glissant, *Introduction à une poétique du divers* (Paris: Gallimard, 1996).

3. Kalevi Kull, "Introduction," in *Gatherings in Biosemiotics: Tartu Semiotics Library 11*, ed. Silver Rattasepp and Tyler Bennett (Tartu: University of Tartu Press, 2012).

4. Jacques Derrida, "Che cos'è la poesia?" in *Poesia: Mensile Internazionale di cultura poetica 11* (Milan: Fondazione Poesia Onlus, 1988).

5. Edouard Glissant, "The Poetics of the World: Global Thinking and Unforeseeable Events," Chancellor's Distinguished Lecture, Louisiana State University, Baton Rouge, April 20, 2002.

6. Andreas Weber, *Biopoetics: Toward an Existential Ecology* (Dordrecht: Springer, 2016). See also Andreas Weber, *Natur als Bedeutung* (Würzburg: Königshausen, 2003), http://www.autor-andreas-weber.de/downloads/Enlivenment_web.pdf.

7. Natalie Knapp, "Die Welt als Analogie" [World as analogy]. Talk given at the conference "Lebendigkeit neu denken": Für die Wiederentdeckung einer zentralen Dimension in Gesellschaft, Politik und Nachhaltigkeit. Heinrich Böll-Foundation, Berlin, November 14, 2012, unpublished. Natalie Knapp, *Kompass neues Denken: Wie wir uns in einer unübersichtlichen Welt orientieren können* (Reinbek: Rowohlt, 2013).

8. Jon Kabat-Zinn, *Full Catastrophe Living: Using the Wisdom of Your Body and Mind to Face Stress, Pain, and Illness* (El Dorado, AR: Delta Press, 1990).

9. Hans Jonas, *The Phenomenon of Life: Towards a Philosophical Biology* (Chicago: University of Chicago Press, 1966).

10. Václav Havel, *Disturbing the Peace: A Conversation with Karel Hvizdala*, translated from the Czech by Paul Wilson (New York: Knopf, 1986), 181.

11. Gary Snyder, *The Practice of the Wild* (Berkeley: Counterpoint, 1990), 74.

12. Parts of this section were previously published in Weber, "Reality as Commons," in *Patterns of Commoning*, ed. David Bollier and Silke Helfrich (Amherst, MA: Levellers Press, 2015).

13. Neera M. Singh, "The Affective Labor of Growing Forests and the Becoming of Environmental Subjects: Rethinking Environmentality in Odisha, India," *Geoforum* 47 (2013): 189–198.

14. Theodor W. Adorno, *Aesthetic Theory* (New York: Bloomsbury, 2013), 85ff.